ELECTIONS AND
POLITICAL STABILITY

The Little, Brown Series
in Comparative Politics

Under the Editorship of
GABRIEL A. ALMOND
JAMES S. COLEMAN
LUCIAN W. PYE

AN ANALYTIC STUDY

ELECTIONS AND POLITICAL STABILITY

A. J. Milnor
Cornell University

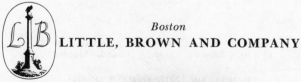

Boston

LITTLE, BROWN AND COMPANY

FOR MY PARENTS

Foreword

The Little, Brown Series in Comparative Politics has three main objectives. First, it will meet the need of teachers to deal with both western and non-western countries in their introductory course offerings. Second, by following a common approach in the analysis of individual political systems, it will make it possible for teachers to compare these countries systematically and cumulatively. And third, it will contribute toward reestablishing the classic relationship between comparative politics and political theory, a relationship which has been neglected in recent decades. In brief, the series seeks to be global in scope, genuinely introductory and comparative in character, and concerned with broadening and deepening our understanding of the nature and variety of political systems.

The series has two parts: the Country Studies and the Analytic Studies. The Country Studies deal with a set of problems and processes deriving from a functional, as against a purely structural, approach to the study of political systems. We are gratified that the participants, all of them mature scholars with original insights of their own, were willing to organize their discussions around a common set of functional topics in the interest of furthering comparisons. At the same time, each author has been urged to adapt the common framework to the special problems of the country he is discussing and to express his own theoretical point of view.

An introductory book, *Comparative Politics: A Developmental Approach,* written by Gabriel A. Almond and G. Bingham Powell, Jr., provides an analytical supplement to the Country Studies. It also opens our set of Analytic Studies, which will offer basic discussions of such topics as political change in the emerging nations, comparative analyses of interest groups, political socialization, political communication, political culture, and the like. We hope these books will prove to be useful and stimulating supplements to the Country Studies as well as points of departure in more advanced courses.

Andrew Milnor's study of *Elections and Political Stability* is the fifth volume in our Analytic Series. It brings theoretical sophistication and a wide range of empirical case studies to bear on a classic polemic of political science, that of the consequences of the principal varieties of electoral arrangements for representation, political system stability, and performance. He carries this issue beyond polemic to the more solid ground of relating the various electoral arrangements to system maintenance and adaptability, given different conditions of social stratification and different structures of political demand. His approach involves the logical derivation of hypotheses from the properties of electoral systems and the testing of these hypotheses in a variety of western and non-western countries. We are considerably closer to having a theory of electoral systems by virtue of his work.

Gabriel A. Almond
James S. Coleman
Lucian W. Pye

Preface

This is a book about elections, but it is also a book about the ability of government to handle problems and to develop policies. Elections are a technique for the generation of these abilities, while at the same time they are one means by which abilities may be dissipated. Some election systems more than others open the way to the failure of a government, by not providing the continuity needed to pursue desirable policy goals, so this book must inevitably be in part about the stability of government as it relates to the stability of the society. Other electoral systems do not provide sufficient channels for divergent interests, and as a consequence they allow representative government to drift away from the legitimate needs of society. In that sense, the book is about representation through the process of election or, to put it another way, about the stability of the society as it relates to the stability of its government. There are a few electoral systems that provide neither adequate governmental stability nor sufficient representational grounding, and they present problems of special interest. But most electoral systems in modern states provide a modicum of both, and when they do they are useful and supportive, that is, they seem to be functional.

Nonetheless, most of the literature on electoral systems has not advanced much beyond the phase of describing the exact consequences of electoral systems of a certain variety,[1] and the advantages of one variety over another. The implication of this debate as societal contexts change has been explored less, especially in the special situations of a society changing faster than its political institutions or of a society that is just entering into the modern world of the nation-state. The concern of this study is twofold: first, to explore the general characteristics of various kinds of techniques for selecting legislatures, including the aspects of nomination, campaigning, and the actual election itself. From this analysis some notion of the functionality of various systems may become a little clearer, and the general relation of various types of election systems to governmental stability may be more easily examined. The second concern is more general and perhaps more important for understanding the functionality of electoral systems. In simplest terms, what general service does any system of elections provide for the whole political system beyond reducing the potential candidates to a suitable number for sitting in a legislative assembly? In pursuit of this question only some suggestions can be made, for a complete answer requires the exploration of the nature of political systems and an understanding of the nature of power.

Central to my whole argument is the concept of exchange in political life. Exchanges are executed between voter and party when the first agrees to support the second for policy considerations. This exchange is for limited duration — the term of the office — and it is general in its scope. For one thing the voter, in supporting one party in preference to another, obviously accepts all that the party will do in office. He cannot give, at least under plurality or list proportionality, one-third of his vote to a party to be used on defense matters, one-third to another party for domestic matters, and the remaining third to still another party because its leader appreciates dogs. He must give his support to one party for one office and accept all that the officer will do in that term. He may hedge his bets

---

[1] An excellent and exhaustive recent survey of electoral systems is Douglas Rae, *The Political Consequences of Electoral Laws* (New Haven: Yale University Press, 1968).

across different offices — one party for president and another for legislator — but within the confines of the single office (or seat in legislatures) he is stuck with whatever that party wishes to do. In that sense, the voter makes an exchange with the party of his choice in very general terms, and it should not be surprising if that exchange is often one of style and tone rather than precisely articulated policy positions.

The prominence of the exchange concept in this volume is based upon a number of sources. Readings of students concerned with exchange theory have been an important stimulus to my work on election systems, especially the writings of Peter Blau and S. N. Eisenstadt. The specific suggestions for bringing the exchange concept to bear on election systems came from Professors Gabriel Almond and Bingham Powell of Stanford University. While discussions with colleagues at Cornell have been most fruitful, notably with Professors Douglas Ashford and Richard I. Hofferbert, a single most important source of stimulation has been one of my graduate students, Steven Norris, whose willingness to read scribbled manuscript has been of enormous utility in honing the concept of exchange and popular participation.

The manuscript has been examined by a number of individuals, and their help has been of great importance to its development. Professor Robert O. Tilman of Yale read the sections on developing states, and Mr. William McClaskey of United Research Incorporated (Boston) contributed substantially to the section on Tanzania. Graduate students at Cornell, notably Mark Franklin, Heng Chee Chan, and Bruce Kappel, made important contributions. The editors of the Series in Comparative Politics, Professors Gabriel Almond, James Coleman, and Lucian Pye, and Mr. John Andrews of Little, Brown, have been extremely helpful, and above all patient, in the step-by-step formulation of this book. Lastly, I express appreciation to Mrs. Eileen Mason for her great care in copy editing the manuscript. To them I owe a very real debt; the book would not have appeared in its present form without their assistance. Needless to say, errors of fact and interpretation are my own.

My wife Catherine has been a source of encouragement and support throughout the writing of this volume. To my parents, who have been patient through the development of a student, I dedicate this book.

                                                        Andrew J. Milnor

Table of Contents

ELECTIONS AND
POLITICAL STABILITY

CHAPTER I

Introduction

ALL GOVERNMENTS seek the voluntary acquiescence of citizens to political decisions. Unless acceptance of decisions is voluntary the state must impose its will by force, and that exhausts resources of money, time, and manpower. As well, the use of force to gain acquiescence restricts the nature of implemented policies to fundamental questions rather than highly complex decisions requiring delicate administration and considerable goodwill. To reduce the political cost of decisions and to retain the ability to cross wide ranges of policy areas, a variety of integrative devices have been used, but the single most common is popular participation in elections. It is through elections that members of a polity have the opportunity to express their acceptance of the decisions of party or elite, and to endorse the formal structure of the political system as a viable method for making acceptable decisions. It is through the electoral system of the modern state that the largest commitment of society to the political system is achieved, through mobilization and representation, participation and popular control.

The character of the systems for choosing governments assumes an importance beyond normal proportions in a period when democratic polities seem caught between crises of confidence in their representative systems and mass apathy over the product of government. As debate centers on various concepts of representation — from classic elites to participatory democracy — inevitably the processes of nomination and election come under scrutiny. The critical analysis may reach different heights, depending upon the interest that is being protected. At the lowest key is perhaps the suggestion that the Liberal party of Great Britain might fare better under some electoral form other than the single-member district plurality form of election; more crucial perhaps is the argument that the same system in the United States is protective of white dominance since its application keeps the number of ghetto-concentrated, non-white Americans in the Congress below their proportional levels. The same argument can be heard in a great variety of societies, developed and underdeveloped, with greater and lesser social cohesion. The question is always, however, the same: whether the method of selecting the governing elite fairly duplicates the character and distribution of society's interests.

The demand for representation of diversity in government creates a counter problem. Insofar as the elite is broadened through the opening of new channels to power, perhaps through the institution of a new form of election, the necessary homogeneity of the elite in the sphere of policy making is immediately challenged. The more heterogeneous the elite, the more difficult the construction of policy coalitions becomes, and the greater the possibility that dissident members will broaden the conflict to the larger society in search of support for their minority views. The end product of pure representation is an elite able to disagree on almost anything, a majority of which is able to defeat any proposal and unable to produce a policy product that will begin to satisfy demands generated from society. The essence of the dilemma of democratic representation is the tension between representation of potentially disruptive groups and the necessary minimum of stability for proper policy construction.

The great debate over the merits of proportional representation and plurality election is in part a debate over which element — representation or stability — shall be emphasized. Product in the form of policy is meaningless (and potentially counter-productive if excluded elements in the society are at all inclined to violence) for the proportional advocate if the exclusion of legitimate interests through the normal workings of non-proportional electoral systems means that policy is made on an inadequate representational base. Representation, argues the plurality advocate, is also meaningless if it is at the cost of any possible agreement among the policy makers on policy, if rather they must spend their time battling among themselves and defeating any hope of consistent, long-term policy lines. Neither side would argue that either stability or representation was totally to be ignored; but each side would argue that its prime characteristic was the crucial element and that an exclusive emphasis upon the other would lead to ruin. It is in this vein that proponents in the literature and politicians in constitutional assemblies pursue their arguments.

The primary focus here is the legislative electoral system of a number of states, democratic and less so. A legislature provides a number of practical services for a body politic, not the least of which are a set of channels for popular expression as well as a filter of diverse interests in which potentially disastrous policies may be caught. Legislators may also be gatekeepers, in David Easton's suggestive phrase, allowing interests into the political process and keeping others, perhaps dysfunctional, out. For government a legislature is in part a testing ground, in part a counter-elite to the executive, and in part co-worker in the processes of maintenance and policy innovation. Obviously, if the legislature can claim to have the true credentials as representative agent of the body politic, then it will have more force and more authority. On a general level the legislature provides advantages that are not available from most other institutions of government. Insofar as it is truly representative of the society, it is able to bring to bear on the executive leadership enormous pressure. By the same token elections for a popular legislature represent to the body of citizens the only practicable method of general citizen influence over policy, and the citizen is through this belief tied more closely to the whole political system. A variant of this argument is also noteworthy. As the legislature increases in power in the society's eyes, it will become a route, an alternative arena, for the presentation of policy claims that may differ substantially from those of the executive. The legislature may have practical contributions to make to the welfare of the governing elite, but as well it represents to the citizenry a potential legitimizer of enormous authority. The result may be a natural tension between legislature and executive, but without that tension the potential for popular disaffection is substantially increased.

Legislative elections are the most prominent technique for mobilizing these legislative powers. In the simplest terms, legislative elections are the means by which members of a significant part of the policy process receive voluntary commitments of support from followers, and the leadership in the legislature is empowered to follow general lines of policy. The periodic nature of these elections prevents legislatures from drifting too far away from the populace and its desires. The periodic nature of elections affects the voter — after all, his commitment is not for life but for perhaps only five years — while at the same time it makes the legislature constantly aware that there is a constituency "out there" and that the pleadings or imprecations of executives must be weighed against those of the voters. The legislature is reminded that it has been empowered and that it will eventually have to ask for a renewal of that mandate.

Executives do not miss this last point, even if their obeisance is mere lip service. Presidents and Chairmen, democratic and dictatorial, have employed the device of the legislative election to sharpen their policy images and to place upon their policy decisions a veneer of respectability that force and coercion cannot produce. As formidable a figure as Charles de Gaulle of France rightly saw the legislative election of 1967 as a potential threat to the image of his policies; the Soviet Union employs every technique internally to produce massive turnout for Supreme Soviet elections, lest the image of popular democracy be tarnished. Developing states, in which an enormous amount of potential authority is invested in president, party, and bureaucracy, go to great lengths to ensure that legislative elections appear to be fair and above board, although by Western standards there is very little for the new legislature to undertake once it has been elected. In all these legislative elections there is a recognition that legislative elections are a form of authorization as well as a means by which popular commitment to the regime may be mobilized. The legislatures may vary widely in power and effectiveness, but it would seem that this function of commitment and legitimization is less variable.

Commitments of the population to support government, expressed through the act of voting for its leadership, lead directly to governmental power, or as it will be called here, governmental capacity. Power, which might be the alternative term, would seem to imply the use of coercion or at least the implication that it stands behind the acceptance of policy decision. The term capacity suggests an inherent ability to pursue policy courses; the larger the capacity, the more complex (that is, demanding) the courses that can be pursued. As the components that create capacity decline in the polity, the shift must either be to a lower level of policy-making or to more direct means. In either case, the political system must admit the inability to generate sufficient capacity to handle problems, and must now move toward force, which will restrict the character and reduce the complexity of the policies it may pursue. The decline in, or redirection of, popular commitment expressed through elections is then directly related to the development of governmental policy capacity; and as a consequence, it is a direct determinant of the efficiency and functionality of the entire political system.

ELECTIONS AS EXCHANGE PROCESSES

In its initial phases exchange is merely the agreement to give support in return for certain rewards. A voter agrees to support a party, and in turn the party agrees to reward the voter's gift with policies that are pleasing to him. There is obviously a second aspect to exchange, for as long as the voter agrees to support one party, he cannot support any other, and thus he voluntarily limits his own options and alternatives.

Third, insofar as that party is also a party which agrees to act within the confines of the government, to accept in short the prevailing political system, the voter is also casting his vote in favor of the political system and against those who would change it. The voter, then, has executed an exchange not only with his own party preference but also with his own political system, and that process of exchange may be vastly important. However the voter perceives his rewards and their relationship to his own role in the state, his performance in the election process integrates him into the state and strengthens the bonds between the state and citizen.

While one form of exchange is normally dependent upon the other, they are conceptually different elements. The first exchange, with the chosen party, is fundamentally an instrumental activity: the citizen receives a reward from the party which he has chosen to support. Whether it be a policy reward, an ideological one, or merely a psychic satisfaction that his party will continue to wave the red flag of the working class, this form of the voting act is most conveniently called instrumental exchange.[1] The other form of exchange, which may or may not flow out of this first exchange, is one of systemic proportions. The voter, casting his ballot for candidates and party of the political system, is also casting his ballot for the system as a whole, validating his own citizenship, and supporting the current form of the political system. If he casts his ballot for candidates that do not share this particular orientation toward the political system, the voter is supporting those who would make substantial changes in the political system; and as a consequence the act of voting is less an endorsement of the prevailing political system and more an endorsement of a party which, explicitly or implicitly, advocates the reconstruction of the political system.

From this observation two hypotheses may be suggested. In the first place, if the voter casts his ballot for parties whose proposals lead away from the political system, his vote be-

[1] The three examples are crude expressions of more sophisticated formulations. Cf. Peter M. Blau, *Exchange and Power in Social Life* (New York: John Wiley & Sons, 1967), p. 238.

comes a form of negative systemic exchange and his particular policy interests become less specific. For example, the voter who casts his ballot for Canadian Social Credit, or the French Poujadiste, or the Nationalist party of Germany is concerned more with the character of the political system and less with specific policy proposals. In that sense, negative system exchange reduces the bond between individual and government, and its prevalence seriously weakens the political system. In these terms, an electoral system is dysfunctional when it encourages the development of dissident parties, by providing easy access to decision making bodies through an over-commitment to representation. By the same token, an electoral system which restricts the representative process to the point that legitimate, functional parties are also penalized encourages the growth of alienation and disaffection from the political system. In both of these instances divergent systemic commitments are encouraged with a concomitant loss of governmental capacity to pursue policy goals.

The second hypothesis does not flow so easily. As the number of negative system exchanges increases, there will be a parallel decline in the number of instrumental exchanges and an increase in the number of positive system exchanges among that part of the electorate still faithful to the prevailing political forms. Whether it be from loyalty, vested interest, or a desire for law and order, the emergence of a threat to the political system increases reaction among the remainder of the body politic. As the level of exchange emphasis shifts from one in which the debate is about the outlines of policy (with concern for the character of the political system a quiet background piece), to one in which the system itself is in question instrumental exchanges decline in favor of system exchanges. The immediate result is a weakening of the policy branches, particularly party and legislature, that seem initially concerned with aggregation, and a strengthening of those branches, such as the executive, that serve as symbols of system continuity. In short, insofar as the electoral system encourages the development of conditions under which system exchange is more prevalent than instrumental exchange, the policy process is subordinated to the defense of the existing political system.

An obvious problem now presents itself. If we assume that instrumental exchanges are those between party and voter, and systemic exchanges those between polity and voter, we are faced with the dilemma presented when the totality of exchanges is solely in one or the other direction; that is, when the totality of exchanges is toward the instrumental side — such as in the case of a party of revolutionary ideology — or is toward the systemic side — in the case of "moderate" parties under enormous pressure from a revolutionary party. The classic observation, made by Professor Maurice Duverger, that a political system is in deep trouble when faced with a totalitarian party of important size on each side of the political spectrum, suggests that left and right become dominated by instrumental exchanges and the center parties become dominated by a sense of systemic exchange, and as a consequence the policy process collapses. At that point, when exchange of either variety becomes the totality of exchange, we can no longer speak of instrumental or systemic exchanges but rather of positive and negative systemic exchanges. Thus, the normal definition of instrumental exchange implies a minimum of systemic exchange; the loss of that minimum is a symptom of illness. It is possible to retain the concepts of instrumental and systemic exchange, however, precisely because of the pathological implications of total instrumental exchange. Total instrumental exchange, it seems reasonable to argue, must include some elements of systemic exchange, positive or negative; in other words, instrumental exchange becomes so dominant that it has become a form — albeit a deviant form — of systemic exchange.

These comments on exchange suggest another, especially with regard to the role of institutions in the policy process. As the relative dominance of government institutions is shifted from legislative emphasis to executive, the legitimation and mass involvement invoked by the importance of legislative sanction is lessened. There are immediate practical implications. A legislature elected on a pro- (or anti-) system platform is not equipped to handle the routine aspects of policy initiation, formulation, and enactment, especially when compared to the normal policy coalitions that democratic states can muster in stable periods. The potential policy packages that the government does submit will be substantially influenced by those agencies able to avoid entanglement in the systemic debate, especially the bureaucracy. There will be almost no innovation since the prevailing mood is strongly maintenance oriented. The inability of the government to accommodate those who have become disenchanted with the political system, the reduction in the authority of the policy process by the devaluation of the legislative branch, and the potential policy conservatism implied by the need to protect the system all suggest a lowering of the acceptability of government and consequently the increased necessity for government to expend its resources on system maintenance by force. The net effect is a lessened capacity of the government to act on policy and a weakened relationship of government to society.

An electoral system which emphasizes representation of a diversity of interests may head off dissidents by giving them needed access to policy makers. The access may then perform both the function of educating the policy makers as well as integrating the potentially disruptive into the political process at a very early stage. But that same representational emphasis may give the dissident a platform he might be denied under less representative electoral systems — systems that compel some sort of policy coalition to be formed in the electoral stage — and from that stage the policy process may be disrupted while the message of the dissident becomes legitimized by his attainment of office. The contrary arguments hold for more restrictive electoral systems. Those systems that tend to penalize minorities may create a stable policy process and force dissidents to join the policy process if they wish any benefits at all. That same exclusiveness may, on the other hand, merely heighten the disaffection of the minority, driving it further from the political system and closer to violent solutions for its problems. In either case, integration or exclusion, the electoral system has played a role in the performance of the exchange, and that role may be a crucial element in the long-range stability of the polity.

COMMITMENT AND CAPACITY

The process of exchange has fundamentally been one of commitments. On the one hand, the party or political system commits itself to certain policies or to certain institutional patterns (neither need, of course, be very specific) while the voter commits himself to support that party or political system. The commitment varies in intensity as well as in its character, but the essential aspect is still some form of mobilization of voter on behalf of policy and government. In that sense the election process has resulted in a resource for the government, a strengthening of its capacity to handle the problems which it faces in effecting the policy process. It is obviously incorrect to suggest that this mobilization takes place for every issue, for it is clear that the daily concerns of modern government are probably beyond the purview of the average citizen. The exchange commitment is a resource, in short, that is of general utility behind general policy lines, although not of immediate application behind each and every policy decision.[2]

Having noted that, it is instructive to examine exchange, commitment, and governmental capacity in societies at different stages of development. In the first place, a society may have few challenges facing it for which government can, or should, have a response. Presumably government decides something in this instance, but as long as its decisions have little relevance to the challenges facing the polity — resulting in demands that the polity might make against the political sys-

[2] The general problems raised by commitment and exchange probably bear on the problems Milbraith mentions in the relation between subject and participant status. Thus, intense participation (which Milbraith argues can be disruptive for subject status) is possibly parallel to the elevation of instrumental exchange to negative systemic exchange. The parallel ends, if the participant is unwilling to disrupt the existing political system, and returns, somewhat grudgingly, to subject status. See Lester Milbraith, *Political Participation* (Chicago: Rand, McNally & Co., 1965), esp. chap. 6.

tem — there will be little need for the mobilization of capacity to pursue policy within the state.

The reverse situation is more critical, for a nation that cannot mobilize capacity through any techniques may not be able to handle demands of any sort and will be assigned by its own people a peculiar place in limbo. Thus, a developing state unable to mobilize its own population behind its general policies, unable to mobilize the necessary system exchanges that empower it to speak as the government of the state, is one of little capacity and of little effectiveness. Consequently the developing state may be unable to do that which its leadership sees necessary. The difficulty is doubly compounded by the essential need for very specific kinds of resources, such as taxes and manpower, which can only be earned through strong commitments between citizen and government.

Perhaps the relation between commitment and capacity can be seen more clearly by examining two cases of low capacity. The first, illustrated by the early histories of the United States and the old Dominions of Canada, Australia, and New Zealand, is the emergence of the state from a period of relatively low capacity for the pursuit of policy, coincident with the existence of a relatively low level of demand. The need for capacity to satisfy demands, or, in other words, the need for the generation of popular commitment is rather low, and with any luck at all the emergence of demands will be accompanied in parallel with the accretion of capacity through commitments. The second case, however, is different. There is a very high level of demand requiring a high level of capacity, but the generation of commitments to the governmental system is failing. Whether this is the case of a developing state with little or no history of popular commitment to the political system, or the advanced state failing to hold popular commitment, the result is substantially the same, and only the generation of new commitments will enable the state to survive. The particular case of the developing state is made much more complex by the tension between the satisfaction of demands coincident with the need for the development of capacity, a tension absent perhaps from the history of the developed states of the West, where these two needs seem by and large sequential in development. From these patterns it is possible to construct a graphic presentation, as in Figure I.1.

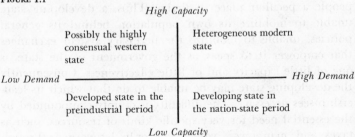

FIGURE I.1

High Capacity

| Possibly the highly consensual western state | Heterogeneous modern state |

Low Demand ————————————————————— *High Demand*

| Developed state in the preindustrial period | Developing state in the nation-state period |

Low Capacity

Immediately apparent is the plight of the developing state compared with its counterpart, the industrial democracy in its historical, preindustrial phase. It is not at all surprising that the emerging states of Asia, Africa, and Latin America experiment with a wide variety of techniques for the mobilization of citizen commitments, ranging from ideology to pan-Africanism to institutional manipulation such as plebiscite elections.

There is no need to assume, however, that once the developed state has reached a certain level of capacity that it will remain there forever. Any crisis in which governmental capacity is inadequate to respond to the demands placed upon it can lead to a downward spiral of decreasing citizen commitment, decreasing capacity, and mass alienation from the political system. As voluntary commitment to the political system declines, force comes into play, adding an even further drain to the already weakened capacity-commitment relationship. The capacity of the state declines, leading to what Professor Talcott Parsons has called "power deflation," and the depressing cycle of declining commitment and decreasing capacity may reach bottom at anarchy or dictatorship. It is certainly worth noting the collapse of the Fourth Republic in this vein, and of course the fall of Weimar Germany perhaps is in the same category. Interestingly enough, in both of these cases of apparent "power deflation," or, in the term employed here, the deterioration of capacity, the electoral systems were highly suspect and the legislatures were unable to provide the necessary governmental response. In the French case a form of election that opened the door to diverse groups in the National Assembly brought about instability between the parties (and within them), while in the German case the legislature was able to mobilize majorities against the political system without being able to support a government of the approximate political center. In both instances the result was a popular will clearly committed to executive dominated government. In neither case is it fair to blame the electoral system for the entire debacle; in neither case can the electoral system be ignored as one variable which brought about legislative instability and consequent policy stagnation.

ELECTORAL SYSTEMS, COMMITMENT, AND CAPACITY

It is not the purpose of this volume to argue that the electoral system is the sole force for the mobilization of commitment. There are other factors of vast influence: ideology, wisdom of leadership, economic and social change, and the whims of Fate. Rather, the thesis of the volume is that a society is suited to make its own choices about the electoral institution by its own character and its own history. But once that institution is established, as is so often the case with human structures, it is often easier to go down with the ship than to change an institution on which a political system so heavily depends. It is certainly fair to argue that the effect of a manipulation of the electoral law to favor a dominant interest might so alienate a segment of the political elite that the cure is worse than the disease, especially if the alienated are long-standing institutions such as parties or established interest groups. Moreover, the implementation of a new form of electoral system might implant permanently the idea of manipulation, and that development in the modern state is one replete with possible vendettas and frequent bloodletting. And finally there is no immediate guarantee that the mind of man is creative enough to construct an electoral system that will bring about the adjustments needed for stable and creative policy institutions. What a poorly designed electoral system may begin, a new and sparkling one may not be able to end.

With these thoughts in mind, it is useful to turn to the electoral systems actually employed by most of the nations of the world. It is possible to detect in them very little deviation from the traditional patterns of proportional representation or plurality techniques, although within these two general categories a vast number of possibilities has been explored. The difference between the two patterns is not difficult to distinguish. Proportional systems encourage commitment through amplification of the principle of representation, by giving as many voices as possible a hearing in the legislative chamber. In so doing, it courts the danger of bringing legislative politics to a screeching halt as the members can agree on only what they do not like and not on long-term policy directions. Proportionality risks alienation or government by bureaucracy (through the failure of the legislative process), both leading to a loss of capacity. Plurality, on the other hand, develops commitment by providing a form of stability in the legislature, by making the citizen a participant in the prelegislative phase of policy coalition building; and it courts the risk of excluding interests from access to the policy process. Again, alienation may be the product as a stable government marches onward to irrelevance. Neither form is absolute in either its benefits to, or damages against, the political system. There are stable proportionally elected legislatures and there are radically unstable plurality legislatures. But the strong pressure of each system is in the opposite direction.

In the final analysis it is the method by which an individual perceives the political system that determines the direction of his choice. If he believes that the use of capacity must be controlled by the mobilization of all possible commitments through representation in the legislature, then he will support proportionality. If his concern is with stability, at the risk of alienation in the society, implying a commitment from a large majority of the population to the political system, he will choose plurality. The debate, then, is about the way in which commitments are mobilized and capacity generated. For proportionalists capacity is generated through representation; for plurality exponents it is mobilized through a relatively stable government able to provide a long-term policy package that is partially prescreened through a coalition at the electoral phase. By choosing between the will of all or the good for many, the individual chooses the nature of voter commitment and the character and exercise of governmental capacity.

THE WILL VERSUS THE GOOD

While the debate over forms of representation is perhaps two centuries old, the central question in this controversy is as old as political theory. Perhaps best stated by the Utilitarians,[3] the conflict between government which emphasizes Will, or expression of interests, and government which emphasizes the Good, or the product of the political process, lies at the heart of the debate over forms of electoral system. Those who advocate proportional representation argue that the Will of all must be represented in the councils of the governing elite, and that a restriction of Will to selected interests, whether through formal disenfranchisement or through the normal workings of the electoral system, is fundamentally out of tune with the principles of democratic government. As soon as the electoral system raises the question of "whose Will" it becomes an undemocratic governmental system precisely because that question implies that some interests will not be represented in the political process. The fact that the political system may not function well, that indeed the political system may not be able to function at all if all interests can find some representation in governing circles, is not the primary question, because the emphasis of proportional representation is representation of as many Wills as possible. Conversely, those who look at

[3] The problems of defining adequately a utilitarian theory of representation are explored in Charles E. Gilbert, "Some Operative Doctrines of Representation," *American Political Science Review* 57 (September 1963), pp. 604–18, *passim.*

the Good, the product, must concern themselves more with the successful operation of government, and thus with a system that tends to reduce the conflict at the governmental level in order that it may be successful in handling the problems facing the state. Thus, the advocates of plurality systems, which tend to reduce the amount of competition in governmental circles, will emphasize more the stability of government and its consequent ability to solve problems.

Those who concern themselves with the Will of interests and those who concern themselves with the Good that government can produce make certain assumptions about societies within which the electoral systems must operate. Those who favor Will must assume that differences within the society are most easily reconciled within the chambers of legislatures, and not in the society itself. Thus, the electoral system plays a much more passive role, merely communicating the desires of the multiple interests in society to the legislature where reconciliation must take place in order for stable, effective government to be a reality. For the advocates of Will the role of the electoral system is the transmission of interest patterns to the government where these interests conflicts will be resolved. Those who favor product, the Good, assign a far more important role to the electoral system. In essence the conflicts must be substantially resolved within the general society, and these reconciliations are transmitted through the electoral system in the form of stable majorities. If stable, effective government is to be achieved, these advocates would argue, it must be done within society and not in the legislature, lest the legislature break down into feuding factions unable to support a coherent program to deal with the problems of society. The most effective electoral system for this purpose is the plurality system, which forces cooperation among warring factions in the society and consequently reduces the amount of tension at the level of government.

Each of these propositions assumes something about the nature of individual societies. On the one hand, the exponents of plurality systems must assume either the absence of fundamental, unreconcilable cleavages or at least the willingness on the part of political parties to ignore these cleavages in the interests of government — in short, a reasonably cohesive social system. On the other hand, the advocates of proportional representation must assume that cleavages in society are so deep and so significant that rather subtle and complex mechanical contrivances are necessary to reflect shades of opinion lest unrepresented groups exchange ballots for more direct techniques.[4] In short, those who focus on representation as the crucial issue in politics are assuming the existence of societies which are not cohesive and are marked by cleavages which cannot be bridged in the society at large. Each set of advocates must deal then with the basic society on which they are preparing to fasten their particular form of electoral system. Those who advocate plurality and the settling of conflicts in the society must court the risk of alienated minorities who feel that there is no recourse for them in the government and thus the only solution is the barricade. Those who advocate proportionality and representation for each interest in society must court the danger of an ineffective, quarreling legislature which is unable to function except as a petulant, negative check upon initiative. Each system has its strengths and each its weaknesses.[5] But in the assessment of the balance between strength and weakness lies the possibility of success for the entire political system.

[4] J. A. Laponce suggests that proportional systems would be most useful where parties divide along communal lines, for example, tribal or religious, and that plurality techniques could be used where parties cut across these lines. "The Protection of Minorities by the Electoral System," *Western Political Quarterly* 10 (June 1957), pp. 338–39.

[5] This point is made quite strongly by Joseph A. La Palombara, "The Italian Election and the Problem of Representation," *American Political Science Review* 47 (September 1953), p. 703.

CHAPTER II

Plurality Systems

> The "more numerically just," the more impracticable, and the more practicable the "less numerically just." One may twist and turn as he wishes; the dilemma remains.[1]

So the German writer Advocatus summarizes the problem that underlies the choice between proportional systems and plurality ones. Plurality systems tend to be the "more practicable" and the "less numerically just" precisely because they do restrict the representation in any given district normally to slightly over half the voters and at the worst to well under that figure. They punish parties of small constituency unduly, unless the party is in a balance of power position in a number of constituencies, while they reward large parties of national following more than their proportional share. On the other hand, though plurality combined with a single member elected per district [2] may seem to be less than fair, it

[1] Quoted in Donald J. Ziegler, *Prelude to Democracy: A Study of Proportional Representation and the Heritage of Weimar Germany, 1871–1920* (Lincoln: University of Nebraska, 1958), p. 98.

[2] The relationship between plurality systems and single-member district systems is only marginal. Throughout this study the two terms are used interchangeably because that is the normal employment of both systems, as the example of England and the number of legislatures modeled after Westminster would attest. However, there are systems where multimember districts are coupled with plurality — Argentina has employed this system — and the much more common system of absolute majority winners in a

is found in those states with the longest traditions of stable legislative government. Whether that tradition is a result of plurality election systems or of the underlying social homogeneity of these systems, however, may yield conclusions about the functionality of plurality as an electoral device.

Critics of plurality systems base their arguments upon its most characteristic feature: for every winner in a constituency there will be one or more parties who get votes but who receive no representation in the legislature. Advocates of plurality systems often argue that since there is only one winner in a constituency, forces across the country will coalesce together until there are only two parties, and splinter elements will have to come together to keep out of power obnoxious, but larger, parties. In order for any party to win, it must be part of the largest coalition in the constituency, and that fact places a premium on cooperation among the smaller groups. So, the argument runs, by encouraging two-party competition on the constituency level, a long step is taken toward the development of national two-party government, in turn providing a majority party in the legislature. It is exactly this process that the proportionalists attack. Plurality systems are loaded gun approaches that say to the supporter of the small party: you cannot follow the politics of your choice, you must vote for either of the major parties or not have your vote count in the makeup of the legislature. The voter is forced to opt for a party that may not be within his range of interest. Further, he may wish to support a party which is outside the general political system in its methods and goals, while the major parties are within a broad consensus. In that special case, unless the small party can gain enough local strength to win one constituency seat, its supporters will have no chance of redirecting the existing political system through legitimate channels. It is difficult enough for a small party with only a few legislative seats; the frustration of a national, but small,

---

single-member district — Australia, the southern American primary, and the French Fifth Republic. However, usually, in debate, single-member districts are assumed to be plurality, and plurality systems are assumed to be single member.

party which cannot win even one seat — though its popular
vote is respectable — is even more intense.

While plurality systems punish small parties severely, they
also tend to reward unduly the single largest party in comparison to the other major national parties.[3] In a plurality
election it is not unusual — in fact it is probably the norm —
for a minority of the votes cast to elect a majority of the seats
in the legislature. If several parties are competing for the legislature, it is certainly possible and quite likely that most
constituencies will be won by parties without any candidate
receiving a majority of the votes.[4] Added up across the nation,
the total for the party winning a majority of the seats in the
legislature can easily be less than half the total vote in the
country. Even further, it is possible for one party to receive
a majority of the votes and a minority of the seats, at the same
time another party receives a minority of the votes and a majority of the seats. Table II.1 illustrates this possibility and

TABLE II.1

| | Constituency | | | |
	A	B	C	Total
Socialists	60,000	25,000	35,000	120,000
Moderates	5,000	26,000	36,000	67,000
Liberals	10,000	24,000	4,000	38,000

all the major criticisms of the plurality system. The disenfranchisement of the Liberal party supporters is complete
even though that party earned a substantial vote. For all intents and purposes that vote is wasted and is discarded. Secondly, a minority of the total vote elected two of the three
representatives because Moderate votes were fortuitously dis-

[3] See, for example, an excellent mathematical formulation in A. Stuart
and M. G. Kendall, "Cubic Proportion in Election Results," *British Journal of Sociology* 1 (September 1950), pp. 183–96.
[4] James G. March, "Party Legislative Representation as a Function of
Election Results," *Public Opinion Quarterly* 21 (Winter 1957/58), pp. 521–
42; Robert A. Dahl, *A Preface to Democratic Theory* (Chicago: University
of Chicago Press, 1956), pp. 148–49.

tributed among the constituencies.[5] Finally, the party which received the most votes, in fact a majority, came in second in number of seats won, simply because the Socialists were unfortunate enough to have votes concentrated in one constituency rather than evenly distributed out.[6] The accuracy of this criticism is testified by the general assertion that throughout the 1950s the Labour party in England had to get 2 percent more than the Conservatives just to win the same number of seats.[7]

These general criticisms are valid. In order for there to be any justification for the system of plurality elections, there must be offsetting goals or ameliorating circumstances that will assume a greater importance than the liabilities. There is the obvious defense that stability is in itself a justification for any form of electoral system and that plurality systems provide such stability. But precisely how far can stability be pursued as a goal if a large, unrepresented segment of the society is becoming less tranquil election after election? Further, what if plurality systems do not result in majority governments but instead produce legislatures with no majority party and governments composed of coalitions? Canada, with one of the longest traditions of plurality voting in the world,

---

[5] While it is the purpose of proportional representation to reduce distortion as far as possible, small districts combined with the single transferable vote can often result in minor distortion. For example, in a three man district 50 percent plus two votes will elect two representatives, since it is impossible for more than three candidates to receive each 25 percent of the vote plus one vote. By the same token, 75 percent of the vote plus three votes will elect 100 percent of the seats. See chap. 4 for a thorough discussion of proportional representation.

[6] Again, while much less frequent under proportional representation, such vote concentrations can work to the detriment of one party. Thus, to take the same three man constituency under the Hare system, only three quotas — which is 75 percent of the vote plus three votes — are needed to elect all three candidates. But if the candidates are of a party concentrated in a few districts where they regularly garner 90 percent of the vote, they will end up with fewer seats in the legislature than they should have.

[7] D. E. Butler and Richard Rose, *The British General Election of 1959* (London: Macmillan & Co., Ltd., 1960), pp. 239–40; D. E. Butler, *The Electoral System in Britain Since 1918*, 2nd ed. (Oxford: Clarendon Press, 1963), pp. 194–97, analyzes the problem in the light of the cube rule.

has in recent years been governed by coalitions or at best minority governments. Finally, how stable can a majority party be if it is composed of representatives from constituencies in which majorities are formed from reluctant followers whose dissatisfaction with the major parties is strong but for whom there are no viable options? Under proportional representation such voters might have a choice, but the mechanics of plurality limit their alternatives. Important questions arise from this apparent disenfranchisement, but before they can be examined — indeed before a plurality system is examined — two questions immediately arise: first, what preconditions are necessary for the efficient functioning of the single-member district; and second, to what extent does the single-member constituency presuppose a doctrine of representation?

PRECONDITIONS FOR
PLURALITY SYSTEMS [8]

Those proponents of plurality systems, who find themselves caught up in the argument over the best electoral system, frequently employ the language and assumptions of the proportionalists. Under the attack of the supporters of proportional representation, the plurality supporters respond in their weaker suits — equality of franchise, absence of gerrymandering — instead of concentrating upon the effectiveness of the choice under plurality systems, resulting as they do in more stability at the parliamentary level and more effective representation of the constituency than with proportional representation. Automatically, when preconditions of plurality systems come to mind, it is generally assumed that equal representation of voters plus equitably drawn boundaries are

[8] Much of the following analysis stems from a reading of Dankwart Rustow, "Some Observations on Proportional Representation," *Journal of Politics* 12 (February 1960), pp. 107–27. The three preconditions are specifically Professor Rustow's although his treatment of the crystallization phenomenon takes a slightly different form. It is argued in our study that marginal voters may not have a chance if one or two conditions prevail: one, that regional distribution gives advantage to one party; two, if the opposition to the crystallized minority is divided. Cf. Rustow, p. 116.

necessities for the successful application of the system. But no plurality system will ever match the equality of franchise of the proportional systems, and it is not wise even to try to demand perfection, because the argument will simply be lost. Further, in placing such emphasis upon these preconditions, others essential to plurality systems will be lost in the shuffle, and the benefits of the plurality systems will never be discussed. Equal representation of voters plus equitably drawn boundaries are important as standards but should not be considered the sole preconditions nor the most important.

The basic unit of the plurality mode of election is the single-member constituency. How it is drawn — its geo-political lines — influences to a large degree who the victor in the single-member constituency will be and thus has considerable impact on local politics although the national accumulation of these disparities may tend to cancel each other. The great controversy in the United States over adequate reapportionment since the case of *Baker* v. *Carr* is a reflection not so much of the inadequacy of the apportionments before that time as of the political sensitivity of the issue. Whereas most of the plurality systems have in the past employed relatively non-political techniques for redistributing population among districts, the method of apportionment in the United States has traditionally been one of legislative decision, and that decision has been made solely by the state legislatures. It should not be thought unusual that these bodies, in the absence of any effective constitutional restraints, tended to favor the interest dominant in the legislature by drawing constituencies in such a way that the legislature would forever favor that interest. A legislature dominated by pea farmers will not usually shrink from underrepresenting urban dwellers and giving the pea farmers in the rural areas more than their share of representation. In the absence of restraints these legislative reapportionments could easily result in allotting major metropolitan areas one or two members of the national House of Representatives while the up-state ruralites might for the same population be given four or five members. The same process prevailed for state legislative districts. Presumably, the malapportionment that occurred would be a clear denial of the equality of franchise, because the urban vote was represented far less than the rural counterpart.

If the first obvious precondition is fair distribution of electors among the constituencies then the second must be a fair drawing of the constituency lines in order that no party may be radically favored. Indeed, it certainly is possible to draw district lines in such a way that all districts may be relatively equal in population but the result will still be foreordained. For example, assume that a state is one-third metropolitan, one-third suburban, and one-third rural. The rural area will probably be overwhelmingly Republican, the metropolitan area Democratic, and the suburbs uncertain, with some suburbs strongly Republican, others strongly Democratic, and still others so changeable as to defy exact categorization. A skillful construction of legislative lines by a Republican oriented legislature will concentrate all Democratic voters in a collection of districts, so that they return majorities of 90 percent or more. By crossing natural geopolitical lines carefully, Republicans are put into districts with Democrats across the state so that the districts become safely Republican but by relatively narrow margins. Thus, Republican suburbs are mixed with Democratic suburbs, and Democratic urban areas may be created with long tails extending out into the safely Republican rural areas. The resulting mix may not be as favorable as the old gerrymander, but the control of legislative representation will still probably be safely in the hands of the Republicans. If the second precondition, the fair drawing of lines without prejudice to either party, is not present, it is certainly possible that elections will not be fair.

But here a caveat is in order. There is fragmentary evidence to suggest that these technical preconditions are not necessarily the most important, provided the divisions in the society are not total divisions of political elements with total programs mutually exclusive of each other.[9] To return to the

9 See, for example, David R. Derge, "Metropolitan and Outstate Alignments in Illinois and Missouri Legislative Delegations," *American Political Science Review* 52 (December 1958), pp. 1051–65.

pea farmer example, the division of the legislature into pea
farmer and non-pea farmer may be clean cut and sharply
divided on issues affecting the pea crop; but on issues with
little relevance to the pea farmer, the legislature may divide
on any number of lines among numbers of different issues.
And, of course, pea farmers able to cooperate on gerrymandering legislative districts may separate even on substantive farm
issues, and such internal conflict may benefit malapportioned
interests. Because the voting behavior of legislative representatives is not limited strictly to constituency concerns, a
single-member district electoral system that is biased against
one social interest does not necessarily result in the total disenfranchisement of that interest. Its influence is dramatically
reduced, perhaps, and its ancillary interests may not be at-
tended, but it is not totally eliminated from the political
system. Further, given sufficient fluidity of voter attachment
to party, the discriminated interest may occasionally find
enough support through the party with which it is identified
to win a majority of the seats up for election, controlling the
legislature, and thus satisfying at least some of its major
problems.

All of this will come about, unless there is over time what
Willmoore Kendall has so properly called the "crystallized
majority." [10] The third precondition, and perhaps the most
important one, is the absence of a significant and nationally
extensive group which votes together all of the time through
an identity which transcends party identification. A crystallized politics is the result of a group of voters which has
developed as a unit, sharply divided from the rest of the
social system and unable either to communicate with it or to
understand its wants and needs. Its representatives are not

---

[10] Willmoore Kendall, *John Locke and the Doctrine of Majority-Rule,*
Illinois Studies in the Social Sciences, vol. XXVI, no. 2 (Urbana: University of Illinois Press, 1941), chap. 8, particularly p. 122. A crystallized
group of voters is quite different from a legislative party under discipline.
The latter are merely under control of a party organization presumably
open to various pressures in the society; a group of legislators representing
a crystallized bloc of voters would be open to influence only from those
voters.

26   *Plurality Systems*

forced to compromise, because they are a majority of the legislature. They are never defeated because as long as the channels of political communication remain open and fair, they
cannot lose. They have no need to go elsewhere for programs
and ideas, because the divided society has produced a political
subsystem which produces in turn all of the dynamics of the
whole system, in microcosm. Opposition becomes divided,
transitional, plaintive, and, above all, futile, because there is
no need for the legislative majority to attend to the interests
of the opposing groups in the system. If leadership of this
segment of the society is united fully behind a program inimical to the interests of the remaining groups in the society, the
whole system can come perilously close to a democratically
sustained, but dictatorial, government. It is difficult to imagine
such a system as a permanent entity, because eventually the
pressures of the minority would become too great. But there
is little question that it can become the primary threat to
democratic politics supported by the most fair and equitable
plurality system possible to construct.

A recent example of a political system manifesting some of
the characteristics of a crystallized politics is the Union of
South Africa.[11] Antagonisms grew between the two language
groups, especially after 1933. While English and Afrikaner
have been roughly equal in population since the turn of the
century, institutions and orientations of the state until the
Afrikaner rise to power were toward Westminster and Commonwealth status. Yet, although institution and society had a
marked English bias,[12] the Afrikaner has his own language,
history, literature, traditions, and economic way of life different from that of the non-Afrikaner, which gave the Afrikaner
an identity quite different from that of the Englishman, a
relative newcomer compared to the Afrikaner's 200 or more

11 An excellent study is Michael Roberts and A. E. G. Trollip, *The
South African Opposition, 1939–1945* (London: Longmans, Green & Co.,
1947), *passim.*
12 Care must be used in the blanket assignment of ethnic loyalties and
roles in South African politics. The leader of the pro-Commonwealth
United party was Jan Christian Smuts, an Afrikaner, as was one of his
closest deputies, Jan Hoefmeyr.

years at the tip of the continent. The Afrikaner sense of unity and separateness is found in his history, one of domination by British institutions and forms, leading first to movement to the interior, then to a savage guerilla war against the English army, and to defeat, occupation, and a constitutional form more British than indigenous.[13] Coupled with a sense that he was a stranger in his own house, the Afrikaner became firmly convinced that he, at least, had no other home; the English could always return to the United Kingdom, the Cape Dutch to Holland, but the Afrikaner had no European home, for his language was unique and his way of life more suited to the platteland of South Africa than to the continent of Europe.[14] Thus, culture, defeat, and a sense of isolation all played a part in the development of nationalism within a segment of the community. Only a political vehicle was needed, and that vehicle was the Reunited National Party of D. F. Malan.

The Nationalists did not win even a plurality of the popular vote until 1958, but they did win a majority of the parliamentary seats in 1948, with a small coalition partner, and then a large majority of the seats in 1953. All this time, during three elections, the party was receiving less than a majority of the popular vote while amassing astounding margins in the parliament at Cape Town. For this development there were several reasons, in part the failure of the technical preconditions. First, there was a relatively equal distribution of population among the constituencies, although the electoral laws did allow a variation of 30 percent between the smallest and the largest constituencies and this bias seemed to be more

[13] There exists a formidable literature on the Afrikaner and his formative experiences. Specific sources that might be mentioned are Eric A. Walker, *The Great Trek* (London: Adam & Charles Black, 1965); F. A. van Jaarsveld, *The Awakening of Afrikaner Nationalism* (Cape Town: Human & Rousseau, 1961); I. D. MacCrone, *Race Attitudes in South Africa* (London: Oxford University Press, 1937). Additional material is cited in L. M. Thompson, *Politics in the Republic of South Africa* (Boston: Little, Brown & Co., 1966), and an older study, Hector Menteith Robertson, *South Africa* (Durham, N.C.: Duke University Press, 1957).

[14] See, for example, S. Pienaar, "Safeguarding the Nations of South Africa," in *South Africa: Two Views of Separate Development* (London: Oxford University Press, 1960).

helpful to the rural Nationalists than to the more urban United party. Second, the constituencies were drawn in such a way that the Nationalists would benefit. In constituency after constituency, the United party would pile up massive victories, while the Nationalists were defeating opponents from the United party by the barest of margins. Thus, the combination of a large number of narrow Nationalist victories with a small number of virtually uncontested United party victories gave the Nationalists the parliamentary majority while the United party captured a majority of the popular vote.[15] The third precondition also failed in South Africa. While the United party was conducting its business as a normal party of broad appeal, the Nationalists were making an election appeal to the bonds that held all Afrikaners together and were uniting them together as a subgroup within the South African political system.[16] Here was an easily identified group, with its own internal linkages, which could support the government in power for as long as it served those subgroup interests. There was no need to turn to any group outside Afrikanerdom because the subgroup could provide all of the support needed for the government. Against this combination opposition has been reasonably ineffective, as it first coalesced in Smuts' United party and then gradually disintegrated into the United party, a liberal party, pragmatic factions, and a rudimentary ethnic union.[17] Since the Nationalist party now

[15] The preceding is taken from Gwendolen M. Carter, *The Politics of Inequality: South Africa Since 1948* (London: Thames & Hudson, 1958), chap. 5.

[16] As early as 1940 the Nationalist segment of Afrikanerdom was moving rapidly toward a reestablishment of the old Boer republic and the return of South Africa to Afrikaner principles. See Roberts and Trollip, *South African Opposition*, pp. 38–41; see also *Cape Times* (Cape Town, South Africa) for most of July 1940. At a rally in Bloemfentein on July 20, 1940, the meeting resolved for a republic "fully in accord with the religion, history, and traditions of the Boer nation." *Cape Times*, July 22, 1940. With Afrikanerdom swinging toward the reassertion of dissident nationalism and the British segment in part concerned with war, the political system was in dangerous waters.

[17] The Liberal party urged integration of the various ethnic groups; the United Federals, a federal system to protect English interests; and the Conservatives, bridging the gap between conservative English and moderate Afrikaner. Carter, *The Politics of Inequality*, chap. 13.

receives solid support from a majority of voters, adjustment of the electoral machinery is not necessary. A firm, crystallized segment came to power in the 1950s, and its high degree of internal identity perpetuates it as a force in the face of political attempts to unseat it.

It is unfair to argue that a crystallized politics is a problem only for the plurality electoral system. It will obviously be a threat under any electoral system. However, a large crystallized segment, evenly distributed, can have far greater success in a plurality system than in a proportional system. In the proportional system a social group may receive more seats than it deserves, but it will receive only minor benefit from this distortion and this will only be an occasional problem. Under the single-member system in a multiparty state, the large crystallized segment can quite easily become a large parliamentary majority able to pursue policies for the subgroup that it represents and without concern for the interests and the desires of the other members of the society. There are no swing or marginal seats to be placated, no pluralist interests outside the subgroup that might swing elections. The crystallized segment retains full control of the system.

The third precondition — the absence of a crystallized politics — is a variant of the problem already mentioned — low social cohesion. It has been argued before that a lack of social cohesion prevents the development of a stable parliamentary majority, primarily because the various representative groups are unable to develop a common ground among themselves for a constructive program; they can be a destructive majority, but not one able to support a government. In a crystallized politics the cleavage is reduced to one deep, irreconcilable dividing force, with all of the social, economic, and political forces present in the subgroup forcing it to be distinct. There may be other splits in the system that prevent any merging of forces for opposition. But there must be one very large segment able to maintain such intense internal cohesion that allegiance to this segment becomes the one force able to master any other division in the society and assume control of the government through normal elective processes. As the one united political force, voting together on all issues against a presumably hostile external environment, it is able to control an otherwise divided and unstable social system.

The absence of two of the preconditions for plurality systems — the fair distribution of electors among the constituencies and the fair drawing of constituency lines — can be rectified through an aroused general public or the intervention of another institution whose powers are capable of being brought to bear on the difficulties with salutary effect. But there can be little hope for tranquillity in the political system if the electoral system, functioning normally, produces a majority in the legislature which rests upon a strong and disciplined large voting segment which will come together on all issues because its internal identity is stronger than any issue confronting it. This malady of the system is incurable through the application of popular techniques because it is precisely the plurality system that keeps the crystallized segment in power. Either the erosion of time or the destruction of revolution will be necessary for the termination of this form of limited rule. It is a political disease for which there is no immediate political cure; and it is a disease which can run rampant in a plurality system because there is no technique for devaluing the influence of even the disciplined large segment under plurality regimes, transforming it into a disciplined parliamentary majority. It is generally true that a plurality system tends to discourage politics of extremism, but in this case the moderating effect of the plurality system may turn about and produce an illness in the system far more devastating in its impact than any general instability proportional regimes are likely to produce.

REPRESENTATION IN THE SINGLE-MEMBER DISTRICT

Preconditions influence the distribution of voter groups within and among the constituencies. They say something about the nature of the district, and by implication about the problems that the representative will have in meeting issues while maintaining his, or his party's, position in the constituency. But once these conditions are met, and any given single-member district is at least roughly equivalent in size, composition, and flexibility to any other, the broader question of the role of the constituency itself in influencing behavior can be raised. It is certainly true that under most systems of proportional representation the tenuous relationship of the constituent to the legislator creates a freedom for that legislator that can be limited only by party or his own ideological commitments. The constituency is able to give few guidelines for legislative behavior because it is not a real entity in either a legal or psychological sense, and the intense relationship found occasionally in plurality systems between represented and legislator simply cannot exist in a multimember district elected on a proportional basis.[18] It is perhaps far easier for the proportional legislator to view his constituency in terms of voluntary social groups than as a constituency in the English sense, because these groups are the only easily identifiable groups in the electoral system. Almost precisely the opposite is true for the representative from the single-member district in most plurality systems, for escape from the parochialism of his district is perhaps the plurality representative's greatest challenge. To accomplish this task, he must apply Herculean educational efforts, his own and his party's labors, and then trust that Fate will do him no dirt. In a word, he is limited, not only by his party and his conscience, but by the boys back home.

Constituencies in plurality systems are real and important entities. First, and most clearly seen in the American case, they are legal entities in a manner only vaguely suggested in proportional systems by the use of general multimember districts. The single-member district has legal boundaries to which the representative is attached — sometimes even by residence — and to which the voter is physically attached through usually rather strict residence requirements. It is from one district and no other that a representative may be

18 Occasionally the relationship produces problems of status among legislators who have no real sense of constituency. See, for example, the problems of Tasmanian legislators as described in S. R. Davis, *The Government of the Australian States* (Melbourne: Longmans, Green & Co., Ltd., 1960), pp. 491–94.

elected; and if he wishes to be reelected, he must do well by that constituency or face the possibility of being turned out at the next election by an opponent who promises more support for the interests of that constituency. As the fortunes of the constituency go, so go his. Thus, secondly, the constituency is also a psychological entity: the representative must feel an identity with his constituency so that he can understand his constituents and they in turn can predict with a fair degree of accuracy his future behavior. If, as is the case with the American practice, there is a lengthy residence requirement, the representative will be intimately acquainted with the problems and prospects of the constituency, so that he can legitimately claim to be representing his home. If he represents the constituency well under these conditions, his future is relatively secure; if he misreads the constituency, his problems will be legion.

The close identification of the representative with his constituency leads to a set of conditions at once a blessing and a curse. First, it gives the representative with clear perception of his constituency interest a set of cues with which he can make the necessary political decisions in the legislature. He has a responsibility that is clear and precise, and he can use that responsibility as a legislative guide and as an index of his own success as a representative. Secondly, the independence of the constituency itself is an advantage for the representative. By using its relative cohesion and compact size, he can defend himself against interests whom he wishes to oppose and who clearly represent a threat to his constituency, even if that threatening interest is within his own party. Third, it is usually true that the single constituency is a manageable whole for the representative, enabling him to follow trends and developments within its confines that may relate to his future electoral success. Thus, the single-member district is generally far safer for the representative than the very large multimember districts occasionally employed under proportional systems, and so it is more likely that an experienced legislature will be the result. The single-member district system gives the legislator advantages — guidance in legislation, defense against inimical interests, safety — simply not available under multimember schemes and certainly absent in party-oriented electoral systems.[19]

The disadvantages of the single-member system modify this happy presentation. While the legislator may indeed have a strong relationship to his constituency, that linkage may serve to restrict him in pursuit of the national interest as he sees it. He is more knowledgeable than his constituents, and he has a much broader view of the world, that of the Capitol and its surrounding environs. The representative will probably face the inevitable conflict at some point during the course of his career, and if it is intense enough, he may be forced to choose between his own local future and the interests of the nation. On the other hand, if he is skillful, he will be able to avoid this confrontation by manipulating the information fed back to the constituency, either by disclaiming any knowledge of the obvious dilemma or simply hoodwinking the constituents into thinking that black is white and white black. No matter how he survives the confrontation between constituency interests and his own perception of the correct course of action, if he employs manipulative techniques, he reduces the purely representative aspect of the system. The dilemma can be further compounded by the importance of party discipline in maintaining a stable parliamentary majority. If party policy demands a position contrary to the interests of his constituents, he can support policy and risk defeat in the constituency, or he can vote as the constituency might require and pay penalties accordingly within his party. One of those penalties might be loss of nomination at the next election, leading to loss of party support, leading in turn to defeat at the polls. Hanged or shot, the trapped representative may wonder whether he is not dead just the same.

---

[19] One of the complaints about proportional representation in Tasmania is the pitting of party candidates against each other, often resulting in the election of independents or hosts of new members who have defeated sitting members too weary to be strong campaigners but strong enough to be experienced legislators. For example, ten of twenty Labour members of the Tasmanian state assembly were replaced in 1946. Davis, *Government of the Australian States,* p. 491.

Of course, constituencies vary, not only in the interests that dominate them, but in their heterogeneity — some constituencies have no dominant interests and are open to manipulation. A representative in a diverse constituency may lose the support of one coalition but gather up the support of another and still win. But to do that, unless there is a rather large independent vote, would mean he was virtually free of strict party ties, and this condition is not a common one. Indeed, even in the United States where party lines are supposedly very loose, it is very uncertain whether this flexibility is found in many of the competitive constituencies, or whether indeed the competitive constituency is not one where party allegiance is the strongest, with independent voters merely forming a balance between two evenly divided pluralities.[20] More commonly, it would be supposed that the representative must throw himself on the mercy of the independent voter and hope that his party's own supporters stay in line behind him, while at the same time attempting to gain the support of potentially disaffected elements in the other party. Here then is another element that can be found more frequently in the single-member district than in the proportional constituencies. While in the multimember constituency it is only necessary for the candidate to appeal either to his party followers or to some mildly irredentist group, in a reasonably competitive single-member constituency the representative must set about coalition building with might and main, in order that he may keep a constant majority behind him. For obvious reasons it is not profitable for the single-member representative to pursue the interests of a narrow segment of the constituency, lest he be caught short against a better coalition builder from another party. Thus, the single-member district forces the

[20] Most congressional elections in the United States seem to have relatively small numbers of true "independents" participating, estimated to be as low as 5 percent in off-year congressional races. Angus Campbell *et al.*, *Elections and the Political Order* (New York: John Wiley & Sons, 1966), p. 197. Samuel P. Huntington has argued that the marginal districts for the American Congress seem to produce the widest differences between the parties. See Huntington, "A Revised Theory of American Party Politics," *American Political Science Review* 44 (September 1950), pp. 669–77.

representative to pursue a moderate course, forcing him away from the disciplined minority except in the most unusual situations, toward the middle, toward a more moderate politics. It need only be added that if the major political organization follows a course of moderation and political integration, the more extreme interests must face ostracism and exclusion unless they are willing to move slightly to remain within the fabric of constituency issues. In the process of representation, a moderate politics does indeed result.

The plurality system embodies within it assumptions about the nature of the political system and the relation of the social system to that political system. As well, it involves certain assumptions about the nature of the representative process that are significantly different from those in proportional systems. First, the direct reliance upon the constituency for electoral support — usually a very large segment of that constituency, if not a majority — forces an identification between the representative and his constituency simply not present in the more diverse and larger multimember districts. That identification not only gives the representative a standard by which to guide his voting in the parliament or in the councils of his party caucus but also limits his freedom in pursuing goals which he may feel to be in the public interest. Consequently, his concerns are much less ideological than those of his proportional counterpart, and much more for the actual care and feeding of the district. He is much more the ombudsman for his voters, since he is so visible to his constituents and is so closely linked to his district. In short, representation under plurality is usually more personal than group oriented.

Of course, the emphasis on personal representation does not mean the exclusion of group representation entirely. To argue that the representative from Detroit is not influenced by the automobile industry, the representatives from the 7th arrondissement are not influenced by the bourgeois mentality, that the representative from Bavaria is not influenced by the Catholicism of the Land would fly in the face of reality. The general proposition surely must be modified to take into account the various dominant interests that may control a region's politics,

wherever there is a dominant interest.[21] The representative in
the plurality system is forced to become a broker in any district where there is no overriding interest; he cannot consistently appeal to a minority in the constituency, lest his
opponents carry off the rest of the constituency and the election. Thus, a plurality legislature will have members of
broader and more diverse constituency politics than a proportional legislature, and the collection of representatives will indeed be more moderate, precisely because of the essential
difference between the two kinds of constituencies. In proportional systems, a multimember constituency ensures election
with a minority of the votes to at least some candidates, while
in plurality systems only a stable constituency majority
will always ensure reelection. That requirement will usually
exclude attachment to any passionately self-identified group,
and will force that group either into the perpetual cold of
opposition •or modify it so that it can become part of a majority coalition.

The nature of the representation process under a plurality
system suggests a great deal about social conflicts and their
resolution. In the single-member district electoral system deep
social conflicts that are not in the form of regional antagonisms
must take their first steps toward solution within the framework of the constituency election itself. This is not to say that
all social conflicts will be settled before the legislature meets,
but it does suggest that deep hostilities will be dampened during the electoral process itself rather than resolved within the
legislative chambers. Indeed, the natural result of the plurality system — sharp distortions in awarding of seats — necessi-
tates the resolution of some of these conflicts lest the system
become radically unstable through the systematic exclusion

21 At the risk of heresy one must note the role of sectional groups even
in British politics. Professor S. E. Finer states, for example, "Some in-
dustries — the motor industry, textiles, and the pottery industry — are so
geographically concentrated that, irrespective of party affiliation, the
M. P.'s form a regional-cum-sectional front." *Anonymous Empire* (London:
The Pall Mall Press, Ltd., 1958), p. 42. See also Allan Potter, *Organized
Groups in British National Politics* (London: Faber & Faber, 1961), pp.
246–55.

from the seats of power of dissident, but important, social elements. The role of the legislature is made easier under plurality systems, because most of the social conflicts that come before the legislature have been reduced in energy through the participation of their group spokesmen in the coalition process. This benefit is not entirely denied the proportional system, but there is a greater tendency in that system for intense conflicts to be represented within the legislature. In short, the modification of conflict is one of tendencies: in the plurality system, the tendency is toward solution of conflict in the prelegislative stage; in proportional systems, it is the legislature which may have to deal with these potent and divisive elements.

While plurality elections tend to produce a moderate politics, social integration subsequent to political integration occurs only in conjunction with essential preconditions. First, there can be no crystallized segment systematically able to exclude from power sharply dissident, but less cohesive, elements. Secondly, the dissident elements cannot be totally regional, for then an analog of the crystallized politics emerges. If the support for contenders in a breakdown of national cohesion is regionally based — north against south, urban versus rural, province versus province — then the single-member district system will have little effect on social cohesion. The contenders then have little need for moderation or conciliation, and little opportunity, since they are coterminous with district lines rather than across lines; and the result will be contending groups that have a secure basis of power and are unable to maneuver toward political stability. If the cleavage is deep enough, the whole political system is in grave straits, and will either disintegrate or at least radically decentralize as did modern Nigeria since the revolution of 1966.[22] There is no electoral system, however, that will be able to put the pieces back together again anyway, so whether this problem

---

[22] The difficulties encountered in the federation are suggested in J. P. Mackintosh, "Electoral Trends and the Tendency to a One Party System in Nigeria," *Journal of Commonwealth Political Studies* 1 (May 1962), pp. 194–210.

applies only to the plurality system may indeed be purely academic. Admittedly, however, if there are dissenting elements in the various regions that do not share the regional antipathy toward the rest, proportional representation may give them a chance denied under a single-member district system, perhaps sufficiently to give some form of coalition of dissident elements in a few provinces plus one or two whole regions the power to govern. The propensity of plurality systems to reward local majorities may deprive the system in these special cases of the possibility of majority government.

Stability in a plurality system may indeed be inhibited by the workings of the single-member district system in these special situations. However, in a society that does not have sharp regional cleavages and lacks any coherent, crystallized politics, plurality systems will usually result in more stable legislative systems than will proportional systems. The ability of a large party to win more than its fair share of the legislative seats certainly encourages the formation of parliamentary majorities that will be able to pursue consistent, cohesive programs and perhaps to lessen the divisive elements in the system by establishing a framework of stable government and a stable environment for the society. Otherwise, centrifugal forces may thrive on the instability and inefficiency of government, leading to their growth in power and strength. One final observation is important. If indeed the plurality system, other things being equal, leads to greater stability of the party system and greater parliamentary stability, in the long run the whole system may indeed be more stable. And if greater social stability is indeed related to, and an outgrowth of, governmental stability, then the divisive forces in the society may eventually be deprived of their raison d'être. Thus, for example, a stable parliamentary government might indeed have had the chance to solve some of the problems of Weimar Germany and might have prevented to some degree the mass unhappiness in the middle classes that abetted Hitler's rise to power through basically democratic means. In social systems in a twilight zone of marginal stability — those between nations like Sweden capable of supporting a stable legislative

majority with any electoral system and nations so divided that
no electoral system will result in a cohesive legislative majority
— plurality systems may contribute to stable, effective government not possible under other, more representative forms of
election. And if the product of more representative techniques
in these marginal systems be ineffective government, who is
represented and how well?

THE PURE SYSTEM:
THE UNITED KINGDOM

The English electoral system is the oldest and perhaps the
best known plurality system. Election is from single-member
districts, with only a plurality necessary for victory. The
House of Commons is large — more than 600 members — and
the corresponding size of individual constituency is rather
small, in 1964 averaging about 44,000 votes cast per constituency. While the party system is centralized into two large
party groupings, there are always a number of three- or more-
cornered contests in which the two major parties are joined
by Liberal candidates and/or one or more minor party candidates.[23] In 1964 the only successful candidates, other than
Conservative and Labour, were candidates from the Liberal
party.[24]

In the election of 1964 the Labour party returned to Westminster with the slimmest of government margins, a majority
of 4 in a House of 630, but with well below an absolute majority of the popular votes. In Table II.2 seats are listed first
as they were actually won, and second as they would have
been divided by proportion of the popular vote. Two results
are clear from this table. First, Labour received a larger margin over the Conservatives than its proportion of the votes
would have justified. Under a system that would have exactly
reflected the mathematical distribution of the electorate among
the parties, Labour would have had only the narrowest of

[23] Note, for example, William S. Livingston, "British General Elections
and the Two-Party System," *Midwest Journal of Political Science* 3 (March
1959), pp. 168–87.

[24] Data for 1964 and for other British elections are from the *Times*
(London) *House of Commons* for the relevant year.

TABLE II.2

Party	Actual	Proportional
Labour	317	278
Conservative	303	273
Liberal	9	71
Speaker	1[a]	1
Others	0	7

[a]The Speaker is usually not contested and is listed under the separate heading.

margins over the Conservatives, and would not have had enough seats to form a majority government.[25] In fact, an unlikely, but logically possible, coalition might easily have put a Liberal-Conservative government in power. Secondly, Labour fell far short of an electoral majority yet it won a majority, not just a plurality, of the seats in the Commons. There was no need for a coalition, because the electoral system had converted Labour's popular minority into the single-party majority usually considered convenient, if not necessary, to support a government in the parliamentary system.

While Labour in 1964 received a plurality of the popular vote and a majority of the seats in Commons, the most surprising aspect of the election is that the Conservatives did not win the majority in Commons in spite of their second place standing in the popular vote.[26] First, it took more votes to elect the average Labour M.P. than it did to elect his Conservative counterpart, since the average winning vote for Labour was 23,935 and the average winning vote for the Conservatives was 23,458. Thus, to win 100 seats the Labour party had to garner 50,000 more votes (at approximately 500 addi-

25 It is not impossible for a minority to form a Government, though it does require the acquiescence of at least part of the remaining membership of the House of Commons. It happened last in 1929 in England, and was recently the situation in Canada.

26 The distortion produced by plurality is a feature of constant criticism, particularly from proportionalists. One of the clearest, though somewhat simplified, presentations of this argument, is in Enid Lakeman and James D. Lambert, *Voting in Democracies* (London: Faber & Faber, 1955), pp. 25–30.

tional votes per man) than did the Conservatives. To put the same data another way, for the Labour party to achieve one half plus one of the seats in the Commons, the party had to garner at least 158,000 more votes than did the Conservatives. This disparity comes out of a second characteristic of the election: the 232 plurality seats, that is, those seats in which the winner got less than a majority of the votes. Labour took only 71 (about 30 percent) while the Conservatives took 154 (or approximately 66⅔ percent). Of the total of 317 Labour seats, only about 22 percent were won by candidates winning by plurality rather than by a majority of the votes, while of the 303 Conservative seats, over half were won by plurality. Thus, a small change toward the Conservatives in marginal Labour districts would have elected a Conservative legislative majority without an appreciable increase in the party's total national vote. It is instructive to examine an example of such a constituency.

The constituency of Ealing North was one of the forty constituencies in which the winner's margin was less than 1,000 votes. It had previously been something of a Conservative stronghold, when in 1959 it had cast 54 percent of its vote for the Conservatives. The vote in 1964, shown in Table II.3, indicated a narrow, but tenuous, shift to the Labour party.

Table II.3

Molloy (Labour)	20,809
Barter (Conservative)	20,782
Wood (Liberal)	6,532

In Ealing North not only did the winning Labour candidate receive less than a majority of the popular vote but he won by only twenty-seven votes over his Conservative opponent. There were ten constituencies like Ealing North, where the Labour candidate won by less than a majority in a three-cornered contest, where the third party won more votes than the difference between Labour and Conservative. From this example a number of conclusions about the English electoral system can be drawn. First, a small shift in votes in just these constituencies would have given the Conservatives 313 seats and Labour 307, without appreciably increasing the total Conservative vote. Secondly, victories by a plurality of the vote, where the winner gains less than a majority, indicate that plurality systems frequently fail to provide immediate constituency representation to constituency majorities. Thirdly, plurality systems are able to change the composition of the parliamentary majority without appreciably changing the percentages of popular vote. In this example of ten constituencies, the total Conservative increase (without assuming any loss in Labour support) would have had to be less than 2,000 votes, negligible in the face of the 27 million votes cast in the nation as a whole.[27] Finally, the importance of even a slightly fragmented opposition to the Conservative party is seen in the role played by third parties in constituencies such as Ealing North. Beyond question a major criticism of plurality systems is that changes in majority control of the legislature can occur with only tiny fractional shifts in the electorate, shifts which play a political role far out of proportion to the actual electoral magnitude.

One other important observation sheds light on the impact of plurality voting in the election of 1964. Three facts are worth repeating: first, the average successful Labour candidate had a higher winning vote than did the average Conservative winner; secondly, the Conservatives won more seats by narrow margins than did the Labourites; and thirdly, the Conservatives won more seats by pluralities than did the Labour party. From this data it can easily be deduced that the Labour party vote was more concentrated than the Conservative vote, implying that always the Labour party would have something of a handicap in dealing with their opponents. Put another way, the existence of single-member districts, no matter how

[27] It can, of course, be argued that a shift of votes in these ten constituencies would have to be accompanied by a national shift of some sort. While swing theories are fashionable explanations of British politics, it cannot be assumed that a shift as small as 2,000 votes in ten constituencies necessarily has to be part of a national tide; it could be sheer dumb luck. The point made in the text is the possibility of such a shift, and not its inevitability.

fairly apportioned, would always hamper the Labour party, because its strength tended to be more concentrated than the Conservatives. In short, the Labour party contested more seats that it was sure to win than did the Conservatives, because Labour strength was not as evenly distributed as was Conservative strength. The Conservatives might indeed not be able to deliver a majority of the country's votes any more consistently than could the Labourites, but the mechanics of the English single-member district system combined with simple plurality victory and the even spread of Tory strength made acquisition of a majority in Parliament much easier for the Conservatives than for the Labour party. It is not a matter of drawing district lines unfairly or of unfair electoral practices, but a matter of the waste of Labour votes. Another comparison is illustrated in Table II.4. In each of these regions the Labour

TABLE II.4

Regional strongholds	Seats won	Percentage of popular vote
Conservative		
Wessex	20 of 21	49.5%
Southeast	30 of 36	51.5
South-Central	21 of 25	47.0
West of England	12 of 15	45.6
Labour		
Northeast Midlands	26 of 28	61.0
Industrial Wales	20 of 23	65.3
West Clyde	24 of 27	56.4

party was the victim of an unfortunate concentration of votes within constituencies of the region, and a system other than plurality would have given more accurate representation to the Labour party in each of the regions classified as Conservative strongholds without punishing the party severely in the Labour strongholds.

The major implication of the English experience is its blatant punishment of parties of limited appeal and its reward of pragmatic competitors. Two assumptions underlie this thesis:

first, the supporters of ethnic or class political movements are most likely to be congregated together in either ghettoes of economic regions within, say, an urban complex; and secondly, those voters other than members of the ethnic or class group who vote for the party will be motivated either by protest or sympathetic attachment. Further, there is a fundamental difference between the pragmatic party, such as the British Conservatives, the CDU in Germany, or the American parties, and parties of ideology, such as the German Social Democrats, the old British Labour party, or some of the protest movements of American history. The middle-class party attempts to appeal as widely as possible while maintaining a reasonably consistent program. Conversely, the ideological party might be described, at least in its earliest periods, as one of intensive appeal directed toward a limited group or class. It is apparent that the single-member district system will tend to punish those parties with intensive appeal, by forcing them to waste their votes in a political form of overkill — it does no good in a plurality system to win by 95 percent, since at most all that is necessary is one-half of the votes plus one, and that is only if there are two candidates (with more than two candidates, even less is needed). While the intensive party is slaughtering a few opponents in its districts, the extensive party will accumulate and transport away the political marbles.

Although it is not the purpose here to wander into the thicket entitled "The End of Ideology," some note should be made of the implications of the plurality system for ideological parties.[28] The parties of intensive appeal may indeed represent a majority of the vote in the country and yet find the going extremely difficult in the legislature against a more evenly distributed party of extensive appeal. The obvious solution is an expansion of the party's appeal that might cost

[28] One can raise the question whether ideology remains a useful tool of analysis. See, for example, Mark Abrams, "Party Politics After the End of Ideology," *Transactions of the Westermarck Society* 10 (1964), pp. 56–63; W. S. Livingston, "The Decline of Party Politics in Britain," *Texas Quarterly* 2 (Summer 1959), pp. 78–92. A counter view is found in Leslie Lipson, "Common Ground and Emerging Conflicts Between British Parties," *Political Quarterly* 27 (April 1956), pp. 182–93.

support in its areas of concentration but that would increase support elsewhere. By following this path, the party surrenders some of its ideological luggage in order that it may acquire votes or, to overstate the case in modern terminology, it moves from a path of extremism to one of moderation.[29] It has been forced into this behavior by the characteristics of the electoral system, and in that sense the electoral system has played the role of political integrator, bringing potentially immoderate parties into the political tradition by forcing a modification of belief. To paraphrase the old saw, if political integration be here, can social integration be far behind? Perhaps it will not be far behind, but perhaps also the party will never be able to tread the road to political moderation if the social system is too deeply divided to allow the party the flexibility which this political shift requires. The nature of plurality would seem to force consensus upon an unwilling party, but a practical view of electoral systems would argue that it is more likely that plurality will only influence an existing pattern of social disintegration rather than eradicate it. The case of England does not yield hypotheses about deeply divided social systems because, it is generally conceded, the tight little island will allow parties of divergent ideology only an occasional jaunt off into the blue. A political system where consensus meets all preconditions for plurality, where a doctrine of representation is fuzzily yet firmly fixed in the popular mind, and where electoral systems are not blatantly placed in the service of government majorities can suggest little about politics in the divided state. An examination of other regimes — multiparty, less consensual, more decentralized — will be a more potent test of plurality and stability.

[29] For a view of a party of ideology in torment note the debates in the columns of *Encounter* in the winter issues, 1960/61.

CHAPTER III

Majority Systems

Simplicity and brevity characterize the plurality election device. With appropriate preconditions and a reasonably settled political atmosphere the plurality technique is one that combines a large measure of electoral efficiency with an adequate measure of electoral justice so that the resultant legislature is at once stable and reasonably representative. In fact, in a homogeneous society the plurality system may be only a contest between Government and Opposition, perhaps with a few minor parties buzzing about the political system, leading to elections which usually involve only two serious candidates. Plurality under these conditions yields a very substantial vote for the winner — or even a majority in a two-cornered, or two-man, fight — and thus satisfies those critics who maintain that plurality may be efficient but often results in victory by only a small minority of the electorate. Certainly, since there has largely been a tradition of two-partyism in England and the United States, plurality has proven itself efficient and representative in the former and in most of the latter.

Plurality breaks down as an electoral device under two special circumstances: when there are too many parties and when there is only one. In the first case, a very large number of parties who prefer warfare to coalition will produce under simple plurality an electoral configuration in which the winning candidate gets a very small percentage of the votes. If there are fourteen parties competing, for example, the chance that the winner will be able to gather in a sizable share of the vote is small indeed, and from that difficulty flows two problems for the democratic state. In the first place, if indeed the electorate is divided into a large number of small political groups, the possibility of stable incumbency declines radically and the inevitable result may be constant instability in legislative representation. It is certainly easier for a newcomer to be elected the first among fourteen than it is to be first of two. In such a divided political constituency the maintenance of tenured, experienced political representation can become a difficult problem, especially if the electorate is given over to whims or faddishness. The second problem is related to this observation. While it is not reasonable to argue that every representative needs to be the first choice of an absolute majority of electors, it is equally unreasonable to argue that representation is fair and democratic if only a small percentage (say, one-fourteenth) of the electorate can decide the issue of representation. In either case, whether it leads to instability or undemocratic selection, the existence of a large number of contenders creates problems not soluble through the normal application of simple plurality election.

Plurality is not acceptable as an electoral device in a situation where there are too few parties, that is, where there is only one party contesting the election. If, as has been the case in the American South for many years and is now the case in a number of independent countries where the independence party has sole authority,[1] there is only one serious contender, the concept of plurality — indeed of election — breaks down entirely. Since it would be asking too much of even the most

[1] In Tanzania, for example, the Tanganyika African National Union won all of the legislative seats, making the state for all intents and purposes a one-party system. The next logical step, conversion to a one-party state, presented the difficulty of electoral control, accomplished eventually through the primary in which two candidates may compete. One of the recommendations of the constitutional commission was that three candidates be allowed to contest, but according to Colin Legum, "this was changed by the Government on the ground that a minority candidate might be elected as a result of vote-splitting." "Single Party Democracy?" *World Today* 21 (December 1965), p. 527.

enlightened political leadership to create another party to provide meaningful competition, the elements of competition
and elite control must come through the process by which
candidates are selected, namely, the nominating process. But
here a major problem occurs. Parties exist in part to simplify
political choices presented to the electorate by placing some
limitation on the number of alternatives; [2] after all, in the
absence of parties there may be a strong tendency for ten million voters to cast one vote each for ten million candidates.
This is precisely the problem presented by multiparty systems:
the absence of loose but accepted structures to limit the number of candidates. How is it possible to limit the number of
candidates so that a large enough number of votes is cast for
any nominee to make his selection legitimate? If there is no
filter to reduce multicandidacy, exactly the same difficulties
are raised in the one-party democratic state that plagued the
state of many parties discussed before.

In either of these two settings the general solution has been
the same, a variation of the principle of plurality, in which a
majority — an absolute majority rather than a relative one —
is required for victory. The actual working has required the
second, or run-off, election among top contenders in order that
the ultimate winner will receive a majority at some time in his
electoral experience. Most systems fall short of this, by declar-
ing a victor in the first election only if he has an absolute
majority of the votes and then deciding the run-off election by
a plurality, as the following example indicates: in the first
election any individual able to raise necessary fees and meet
requirements is allowed to enter in open competition; following this election within a stated period there is a second
election between the top contenders, or between all serious
contenders (usually those who gained above a certain percent on the first ballot, for example, 5 percent), and the winner is the one with the most votes. In systems where the
competition is between only the top two, there is guaranteed
an absolute majority for the winner; in systems where there is

[2] Cf. Sigmund Neumann, *Modern Political Parties* (Chicago: University
of Chicago Press, 1956).

only a required minimum in the first balloting to qualify for
the second, there is usually a winner by a large plurality, although, as shall be seen in the French Fifth Republic, which
uses a percent minimum,[3] it is not unusual for the second ballot to be between only two candidates. Between the first and
second ballotings coalition building and realignment usually
take place eventually resulting in a pattern not unlike pure
plurality systems. Whether or not the stability of standard
plurality devices is achieved, majority systems are devices that
reduce a large number of candidates to one individual who
has at least a large plurality of the vote, if not a majority.

THE SOUTHERN PRIMARY

The run-off is a device which is most commonly found in
systems where there is little opportunity for a winner to
achieve a large enough segment of the vote the first time
around. Thus, it is a device for bestowing legitimacy, since the
final winner will have received a majority or at least a large
plurality somewhere along the electoral line; and no winner
will be elected by a small, albeit the largest, fraction of a total
vote divided among many contenders. In that sense it is a
technique useful in decentralized social systems where the
possibility of large numbers of significant contenders is very
real, as in the southern states of the United States where the
dominance of the Democratic party has assured the winner of
the Democratic primary victory in the general election the
following November. At the same time most of these state
Democratic parties — since by and large they were the only
party contesting state elections seriously — have been so large
that they were unwieldy and faction-ridden, unable to discipline themselves and to impose any restraint on multiple
candidacy. In order to prevent primary nomination — and
therefore almost assured election — of a candidate who had
never received a large share of the popular vote, a second
primary was required for the top contenders. Thus, while the

[3] At first, the minimum vote percentage for admission to the second
ballot was 5 percent; for the elections of 1967 the minimum was raised
to 10 percent.

electorate might not get their first choice, at least the voters in the Democratic primaries had the opportunity in the second primary to decide which of the more important contenders they desired to make their nominee. Supporters of candidates the first time around who were unable to make the second election would have to decide which of the remaining candidates fitted their interests the best. This process became one of political integration, allowing an electorate too disorganized to make a selection from among candidates in open competition to come to some acceptable decision from among a restricted list.[4]

Nonetheless, while it has been apparent throughout this analysis that plurality exercises a restraining influence on the number of contenders, it is worth asking whether the addition of the run-off ballot does not have something of the opposite effect. The argument applied to the southern United States is perhaps best stated by V. O. Key, Jr.

> . . . If the man with the largest number of votes takes all, no matter how small a proportion of the total vote they may be, the incentive of political leaders and sub-leaders is to try to maneuver into a winning combination in the first primary. On the other hand, if there is a second voting a candidate can take a chance that his support — no matter how weak it may be — will be enough to place him first or second, with an opportunity to run in the final sweepstakes.[5]

At the time of Key's observations the characteristics of southern politics were well known. There was only one party that counted at the state level, the Democratic, and the party's candidates usually were assured victory in the general election. There was, however, as seen in the Texas case described below, factional disunity in almost all southern Democratic

---

[4] This is not to suggest that primary nomination is an adequate substitute for party competition but only that it is more democratic than scatter-gun competition or no competition at all. Cf. Allan P. Sindler, "Bifactional Rivalry as an Alternative to Two-Party Competition in Louisiana," *American Political Science Review* 49 (September 1955), pp. 641–62.

[5] *Southern Politics in State and Nation* (New York: Alfred A. Knopf, 1950), p. 420.

parties providing the possibility for multiple candidacy at the first primary election. In order to assure mass popular approval of the candidate, the run-off became an absolute necessity.

In a multifactional situation, there is little question that the run-off technique tends to encourage a vast number of candidates. In Florida in the 1930s and 1940s,[6] for example, Key notes that between seven and fifteen gubernatorial candidates contested the Democratic primary regularly, with the top candidate receiving less than a third of the vote and occasionally as low as a sixth.[7] Perhaps, however, the stronger evidence is found in the state of Texas, which changed the primary from a simple plurality victory in 1908–16 to a second-ballot system involving the top two contenders. The change in the number of primary candidates was marked. Before 1916 the average number of candidates in the Democratic gubernatorial primary was 2.6 per primary, and only one candidate in the five elections received less than 5 percent of the votes. Between 1916 and 1948, however, the average number of candidates was 7.4 per primary, and almost five candidates per primary received less than 5 percent of the total vote.[8] In these two states of the American South, there is little question that the existence of the run-off primary raises the hopes of contenders whose strength is not sufficient to carry a normal plurality election.

In parts of the American plurality system the demands of electoral justice have taken a turn toward the pursuit of an absolute majority of the votes cast. In the absence of viable two-party competition or at least some pressure toward a small number of candidates, there remains the possibility that the nominee selected in the direct primary — and the consequent winner in the general election — might have the support of less than a majority and probably less than a large plurality. In the process of creating a new electoral form, the run-off primary, southern states without strong factional discipline

---

6 Described by Professor V. O. Key, Jr., as "Florida: Every Man for Himself."

7 *Southern Politics*, pp. 88–89.

8 *Ibid.*, p. 421.

have created a situation where initial multicandidacy seems to be the order of the day, until either a competitive party structure emerges or factional discipline is dramatically increased. Parallel with the southern experience, there seems little question that the staying power of many of the French smaller parties is based upon the bargaining power that they are able to develop between the first and second elections. Indeed, the additional element of the French run-off election — entry to the second election is from those who achieved more than a set percentage on the first ballot rather than solely the top two — would seem to strengthen the hand of the minor party wherever it was able to exceed the rather small minimum number of votes. Nonetheless, offsetting this apparent encouragement for multipartyism in the French case is the nature of the contenders: in the American South the contestants may belong to some very loose factional structure, though they probably do not; but in France the candidates are part of a party structure — no matter how loose — and that might imply some long-term attachments as well as some organizational discipline.[9] From this line of argument an hypothesis emerges: while loose, personal factions might not be affected by the pressures toward coalition found in the run-off system, a multiparty system, even one as casual in its centralization as that of France, might develop long-term working relations among the parties as a result of the pressure toward coalition which might in turn eventually lead to a decline in the total number of competing parties. In simplest terms, it might take very great effort to bring order out of a system of loose, personal factions, while less effort might be required to bring about order in a decentralized party system. In examining the run-off ballot of the French Fifth Republic this hypothesis must be kept in mind lest it be assumed that the dynamics in the two cases of the American South and de Gaulle's republic are the same.

[9] Indeed, between the time of the first and second ballots of the 1967 legislative elections the pages of *Le Monde* contained evaluations of the discipline within the various contending parties as they decided who would contest the second ballot. *Le Monde* (Paris), March 7–14, 1967, *passim.*

FRANCE, 1951 —
THE APPARENTEMENT [10]

In the pursuit of a better electoral system there are few countries with the experience of France. But before discussing the experience of the Fifth Republic (1958–   ), it is useful to examine the single most complex electoral system employed in recent French legislative elections, the *apparentement,* devised for the occasions of the 1951 and 1956 National Assembly elections. With the apparentement the parties of the Fourth Republic (1946–58) were given, by law, the right to form coalitions that would result in an absolute majority on the first ballot, obviating the need for any further distributive principle, in this particular case not a run-off election but the distribution of seats by proportional representation. The general purpose is the same as that of the run-off, since if no party receives an absolute majority of the vote on the first ballot, there will be a distribution of seats by proportion of the vote cast, thus ensuring that each contending party receives roughly its share of the vote. Such an effort to ensure rough electoral justice in the absence of an absolute majority behind any party would fail unless there was more than one seat up for election from any single constituency, in this case all of the seats from one department in France. The system as devised made the second ballot unnecessary, while at the same time it encouraged the same general kind of coalition building among the smaller contenders that is characteristic of single-member constituencies employing the run-off principle between the first and second ballot. Given the multimember constituency such a device might be most effective as a coalition-building system except for one problem: while the single-member district encourages coalitions behind one win-

10 A general description of the apparentement as well as the other electoral techniques used in France during the Fourth Republic and the beginning of the Fifth is found in Jean-Marie Cotteret, Claude Emeri, and Pierre Lalumiere, *Lois electorales et inegalites de representation en france, 1936–1960,* in Cahiers de la Fondation Nationale des Sciences Politiques: partis et elections, no. 107 (Paris: Librairie Armand Colin, 1960), esp. pp. 304–19 for the apparentement.

ner, who then represents that coalition in the legislature, in a multimember district it is more than possible that an electoral coalition might be forged out of hostility to one enemy, defeating that enemy in the election but creating no lasting coalition in the legislature.[11] That difficulty and the eventual inability of the center parties to come together in effective electoral coalitions at all led most certainly to the discrediting of the French apparentement of the Fourth Republic.[12]

The electoral system desired by the government coalition for use in the French elections of 1951 had only one general purpose: to protect the center parties of the government from the emergent extremes of the Communists on the left and the Rally of the French People (RPF), supporting General Charles de Gaulle, on the right. Since the purpose was clear, a number of general varieties of electoral systems was excluded from consideration since their application would benefit the extreme parties. As importantly, the electoral distribution of the center parties apparently made no one system satisfactory for the entire country. For example, although the parties of the center were strongest in the rural areas, to the point of being a majority in some rural departments, they were weak in the Paris region where the Communists might be expected to carry the working class while the Gaullists would do very well among the middle classes.[13] Thus, the limitations were clear: proportional representation could not be used, since no party, includ-

----

[11] This is the contention in Jean Bruyas, "La Loi du 9 mai 1951 relative a l'election des membres de L'Assemblee nationale," *Revue du droit public et de la science politique* 67 (October–December 1951), pp. 1069–77; the same theme is found in Philippe Biays, "L'Apparentement des listes electorales," *Revue du droit public et de la science politique* 70 (April–June 1954), pp. 438–64.

[12] In 1956, the second election under apparentement, there were more alliances but only eleven departments had alliances sufficiently strong to win the majority. Peter Campbell, *French Electoral Systems and Elections Since 1789* (Hamden, Conn.: Archon Books, 1965), pp. 125–26.

[13] Campbell, *French Electoral Systems*, pp. 113–23, esp. the tables on p. 121; a general description of the problem of reform as seen from the party perspective is R. G. Neumann, "The Struggle for Electoral Reform in France," *American Political Science Review* 45 (September 1951), pp. 741–55; François Goguel, *France Under the Fourth Republic* (Ithaca, N.Y.: Cornell University Press, 1952), pp. 66–78.

ing the coalition of the center, would probably have a majority of the votes. The same could be said of single-member districts in which the Communists and the Gaullists might easily defeat the parties of the center, unprotected by coalition. Finally, the extremist vote in Paris and its environs had to be neutralized or at least reduced. The election system derived for the French Republic in 1951 is eloquent testimony to the proposition that for any political problem a suitably biased electoral system can be created.

The French electoral technique of 1951 had not one, but at least three, different forms. First, the basic system used in all parts of the country except in Paris and its immediate surroundings was a form of proportional representation that tended to favor the largest parties and that the center coalition felt would be advantageous in rural areas. In the Paris region (the departments of the Seine and Seine-et-Oise) a different form of proportional representation was employed that would give slight advantage to the smaller parties, which the center coalition parties felt they would be in the Paris region. (The first is called list proportional representation under the d'Hondt system, the second list proportional representation under the largest remainder system.) [14] The distortions of each electoral technique would work to the advantage of the center coalition and consequently offset the power of the extreme parties. The third electoral form was specifically designed to frustrate the proportional aspects of the electoral system. Outside the Paris region any parties which wished to could employ the apparentement, combine into alliances and be treated as one party in the counting of votes; and should that alliance win a majority of the votes in the department, it would win all the seats in the department. Only if there were no alliance or single party gaining an absolute majority would the proportional representation system be applied. In departments where an alliance between parties won an absolute majority of the votes and thus all the seats, the distribution

---

[14] See Enid Lakeman and James D. Lambert, *Voting in Democracies* (London: Faber & Faber, 1955), chap. 5 for a brief definition of these terms.

among the members of the alliance would be by proportional representation of the d'Hondt method. The system would be proportional representation only as long as no alliance could earn a majority of the departmental vote; the more successful the alliances, the more the system would approximate majority elections.

The apparentement would function as its designers intended only if three conditions prevailed: first, that the parties of the extremes remained relatively isolated and were unable to form electoral alliances of their own; second, if the center parties were able to reduce their internecine warfare sufficiently to make the alliances possible; and, third, that the center coalition win enough seats in the provinces to offset the grievous losses that they might expect in the Paris region. Although the requirements were not completely satisfied in 1951, the electoral system performed satisfactorily for the center parties. The center coalition was not sufficiently united to form alliances in all the constituencies, and the Gaullists were able to form some, but nonetheless a large number of successful center alliances were made. In only twelve of the ninety-five departments no alliances contested, although in seven of the departments two separate alliances were formed. The RPF formed thirteen, leaving the remainder mostly to the center parties. The success of the alliances was mixed, as in one department one party won all by itself, and thirty-nine departments were won by alliances of two or more parties. Although the practice of alliance building was less than absolutely effective, it did serve its purpose: the parties of the center gained a bare majority (51 percent) of the vote while gathering over 60 percent of the seats in the chamber. The extremes were penalized, though the Communists more so than the Gaullists.[15]

Proportional representation with the addition of the apparentement comes close to being proportional representation

[15] A brief analysis of the kinds of alliances formed and of the conjectured nature of the Assembly had other electoral systems been used are found in Peter Campbell, "Remarques sur les effets de la Loi Electorale Francaise du 9 Mai 1951," *Revue francaise de science politique* 1 (October–December 1951), pp. 498–502.

in form while plurality in fact. First, there is the obvious fact that the "winner take all" aspect of apparentement is hardly proportional and is not in any sense derived from any application of the principle of proportional representation. Secondly, there is the severe distortion that may result from the application of the majority principle, especially against groups unable to create alliances of their own. The Communists, for example, gained 24.8 percent of the vote in provincial France while winning only 16.0 percent of the seats.[16] But the major departure from proportionality implicit in the use of apparentement is the emphasis upon electoral coalition construction. The temptation — in fact, the obvious encouragement — is to construct electoral coalitions before the voting in order to reduce the number of competitors. Electoral coalitions are not usually totally pragmatic, for they involve delicate negotiations about candidacies and policies sufficient to cast severe strain on any but the most eager parties. (The fact that in the face of an apparently severe threat from the extremes of French politics the center parties were still unable to forge electoral coalitions in twelve or more departments suggests the difficulty involved.) Nonetheless, the system of apparentement encourages the reduction of interparty warfare before the election; in that sense it adheres to the principle of plurality election and seriously defeats the general purposes behind proportional representation. The majority vote, distortion in the translation of votes to seats, and the emphasis on coalition building all attempt to produce a legislature more unified than the population and less a mirror image of the society itself.

ELECTIONS IN THE FIFTH REPUBLIC

Things are much more complicated today. The events of the summer of 1951 demonstrated as clearly as possible that the composition of the parliamentary majority changes with each problem before Parliament. On religious or educational questions there is a majority of the Right, in the old sense of the word, which includes the RPF, the Moderates, the MRP, and

[16] Campbell, *French Electoral Systems*, p. 121.

some Radicals, and a left-wing minority, including the Communists, the Socialists, and most of the RGR. But in neither camp
do the various parties agree among themselves on any other
question. If the issue involves political institutions, a general
outlook at once extremely hostile to what the Communists call
"popular" democracy is adopted by the Center majority. . . .
But the various elements of this majority, agreed on what they
do not want, are far from equally agreed on what they do
want.[17]

The political structure of France in the early fifties was torn
apart by cleavages that ran deep within the social system itself,
and around which parties, or at least groups of factions, were
able to unite. If politics of the Fourth Republic could not be
described in the context of the French revolution, France's
population could at least be charged with continuing struggles
of the nineteenth century well beyond their due date of burial.
The political implications of the decentralization of French
society are found most clearly in the constant inability of
the French system during the Third and Fourth Republics to
produce a strong, stable parliamentary majority. Instead,
chambers were composed of several basic groups of varying
numbers of parties which might or might not choose to support the government in power, indeed even the institutions of
government themselves. Throughout the period of the Fourth
Republic, no single electoral system seemed to hold the favor
of any consistent majority, although proportional representation with strong overtones of plurality was common.

Since 1958, when the constitution of the Fifth Republic was
adopted, an apparent change has come over the casual anarchy of pre-Gaullist France. France has tried to settle many
of the major issues of the Fourth Republic, has strengthened
its international position with the creation of a nuclear force,
has vastly increased its role in Europe, and has created something of a minor miracle by seeming to provide an elected
government which can pursue policies over time without the
constant fear of governmental crisis. Since the beginning of
the Fifth Republic it has had a relatively stable, if somewhat

[17] Goguel, *France Under the Fourth Republic,* p. 138.

restive, legislature, whose most remarkable feature has been
the presence of a reasonably stable, almost moderate, party
with a very large share of the seats in the Chamber.[18] These
political changes have occurred coincidentally with two general developments in France: first, the institution of a restrictive plurality system of elections with severe penalties for
minor parties without adequate local strength; and second,
the emergence of a new social system based around a French
middle class.[19] These two factors, combined with the tendency
at the presidential level for parties to polarize around pro- or
anti-Gaullist sentiment, have seemed to force some stability
upon the French political scene.

A growing sense of French unity has caused the decline in
influence over the past decade of the extremist parties leading
in turn to solutions for some of the basic divisive problems in
the society — for example, the attempted solution to the religious education question by the Debre formula [20] — which

[18] Perhaps as important, the UNR seems to be a party of modernity,
"unencumbered by the traditional ideological burden, it can be all things
to all men." D. B. Goldey, "The French Referendum and Election of
1962: the National Campaign," *Political Studies* 11 (October 1963), p. 307.

[19] While it is comforting to argue that an increasingly affluent society
results in a moderate politics, it is neither necessarily true nor essential to
the argument. See, for example, Richard F. Hamilton, *Affluence and the
French Worker in the Fourth Republic* (Princeton, N.J.: Princeton University Press, 1967), who argues that the French worker remained left
while increasing his worldly goods. On the other hand, de Gaulle does
seem to have strength in the modern areas of France, "the richest, most
industrialized, most populous parts of the country." D. B. Goldey, "The
French Presidential Election of 5 and 19 December 1965: Organization and
Results," *Political Studies* 14 (June 1966), p. 213. Further, Philip Williams
notes that there might be some erosion in the left loyalties of Hamilton's
affluent radical workers. De Gaulle's support among workers was lower
"than in other classes, but still quite substantial" in the election of 1965;
the Communists were unable to "retrieve those lost to de Gaulle in 1958."
"The French Presidential Election of 1965," *Parliamentary Affairs* 19
(Winter 1965/66), pp. 25, 27.

[20] See, for example, Bernard E. Brown, "Religious Schools and Politics
in France," *Midwest Journal of Political Science* 2 (May 1958), pp. 160–78.
Suggesting the decline of the religious issue — a seemingly necessary step
toward a union of moderate and left — is the response of M. Maurice
Faure to a 1962 anticlerical heckler: "I pity you if you're still stuck on
that!" Quoted in D. B. Goldey, "French Referendum and Election of
1962," pp. 300–301.

will, when successful, lead to a greater sense of unity. The growing influence of modern France in the industrial and managerial segment of the economy further stabilizes the regime, particularly because it was in these areas that opposition to the old parliamentarism of the Fourth Republic was apparent.[21] Additionally, the decline in intensity of Communist alienation as a result of the thaw in the Cold War has brought the party in closer to the center while at the same time prosperity has made it more obsolete as a protest device. The nation's increased international role and very real strides in nuclear and technological phases have fostered a sense of national identity and spirit. Finally, there is General de Gaulle himself, the one national figure around whom polarizations might occur.[22] De Gaulle's presence provided a center for advocates and a symbol for opposition that transcended the divisive controversies which so paralyzed parliamentary government in earlier republics.

Coincident with these centralizing tendencies in the French social system was the electoral system of the new republic. Prior to the Fifth Republic, the electoral system was a variation of list proportional representation, the apparentement, allowing a party or coalition of parties with very strong local support to win all the seats in a department if it achieved a majority of the popular vote. Proportional representation as a principle was rejected for the new government and a variation of the single-member district system was adopted, requiring an absolute majority for election on the first ballot, with only a

[21] It is worth noting that the Gaullists seem much the stronger in the larger departments in the legislative elections of 1962, while the traditional parties of the Fourth Republic seem to have their strength in the smaller departments. Further, the combined Gaullist-Communist vote in the seventeen most industrialized departments (see Goguel, *France Under the Fourth Republic*, p. 113) was higher than in the rest of France for the referenda and legislative elections of 1958–62, suggesting that protest against the Fourth Republic was higher in modern France than in the traditional areas of the country. This pattern is, however, mixed, although it could be the result of the addition of more industrialized departments to Goguel's list of seventeen.

[22] This is the argument of Hugh Thorburn, "The Realignment of Political Forces in France," *International Journal* 19 (Autumn 1964), pp. 486–95.

plurality necessary for election on the second ballot conducted one week later. Between first and second ballot, candidates would be eliminated who had achieved less than 5 percent of the popular vote.[23] Additionally it was expected that a number of hopeless candidates would withdraw voluntarily, so that the second ballot would be a straight fight between two major contenders, or at least there would not be a large number of contenders per constituency the second time around.[24]

The adoption of the run-off ballot seemed necessary in France in 1958. In the preceding election of 1956 there were at least fourteen major groups or parties contesting the election — although in different departments alliances were created — and of the fourteen, thirteen achieved representation. Of the 543 seats from France proper the largest party, the Communists, gained only about 25 percent of the seats while two others gained about 18 percent each. Thus, the electoral system of the Fourth Republic not only allowed a large number of competitors but also rewarded a large number of parties with seats in the legislature.[25] Obviously, in a divided political system a single-member district system such as that in the United Kingdom would at the same time be unjust and might not produce a legislature much more united than that produced by proportional representation. While few of the parties had any national strength, each was strong enough in some district to attract a plurality of the voters and, consequently, to elect some member from somewhere in France.

23 Changed to 10 percent for the election of 1967.

24 The ideal contest would probably be between one of the Gaullist candidates and a Communist candidate, thus assuring a strong legislative majority for the President and the defeat of the Communist. The purpose, then, was roughly the same as that of 1951, as noted by Raymond Aron: "I should add that the composition of the last Assembly (elected in 1956 under the law of 1951) was largely the result of a mistake, because any French politician knows that in a nation where, let us say, 30 to 40 percent of the people vote for extremist parties, you must have an electoral system which reduces their representation." *France: The New Republic* (New York: Oceana Publications, 1960), p. 37.

25 As has been noted, the electoral system of 1951 was not supposed to work that way; but, as will be seen in the case of the electoral device for the Fifth Republic, electoral systems do not always seem to work the way they are supposed to. See Appendix 197–9.

In a disorganized political system resting upon a decentralized social system, the only apparent variation of the single-member district system would be one utilizing the run-off principle. In the first election the disorganized political system would have its run, allowing as many candidates as could post the rather stiff filing fee, giving small parties the chance for survival as bargainers. The second ballot would then select from among the truly serious contenders the winner.

While it is surely true that the intention of the run-off ballot principle is twofold — first, to give the disorganized political system its run of candidates, and second, to reduce these down to manageable proportions — there is often a discrepancy between the intention and the reality. The unhappy experience of the electoral system of 1951 as it worked in 1956 served as an example for the planners of the Fifth Republic. By and large the elections since 1958, as illustrated in Table III.1, have followed form as well as, if not better than, might be expected. The number of candidates elected on the first ballot

TABLE III.1

Year	Seats	Candidates	Per seat
1958	465	2800	6.02
1962	465	2400	5.16
1967	485	2200	4.54

did not change substantially between 1962 and 1967, but they did change markedly between 1958 and 1962, when the number of first-ballot victors were 39 and 96, respectively. Most importantly for the analysis here is the interaction between the two general patterns of change: the long-term polarization of the political system, reflected in declining numbers of candidates and the increase in the number of first-ballot victories; and the short-term polarization occurring between the first and second ballot at any given election. If short-term polarization did not change relative to the overall change in polarization, then perhaps forces other than the electoral system might be examined; but if the short-term polarization is much greater than the long-term polarization at any given election, then it might be argued that the second-ballot system provides a unique opportunity for polarizing forces to accelerate their efforts.

Any analysis, even the most cursory, would indicate that the electoral system has provided that opportunity. Two measures may be adopted to test how effectively the parties used the second ballot. First, the number of candidates participating in the second ballot indicates that the electoral system seemed to serve large parties quite well, since the number of candidates declined from about 1300 in 1958 to about 860 in 1967, even though the number of first-ballot candidates in the two elections did not decline as sharply. The second test is much more crucial and indicates the extent of the polarization. In 1958 about one-fifth of the seats were "straight fights," usually between a Communist and a Gaullist; in 1962 there were 203 straight fights out of a possible 369 constituencies, about 65 percent; in 1967 there was a straight fight in 335 of a possible 398, about 84 percent. In 1958 there were three candidates in about half the second-ballot contests; in 1967 there were three in only about 15 percent of the constituencies. The alliance of the left — between the Federation and the Communists — provided more than 75 percent of contests against a Gaullist candidate in the 1967 second ballot. With little question, then, it can be argued that the electoral polarization around a Gaullist group and an anti-Gaullist, leftist group has emerged, in part because the electoral system enables such bargaining and negotiation, in part because the plurality aspect of second-ballot victory requires it.

The beginnings of a new stability in French legislative politics have not been without cost. The electoral system is restrictive, penalizing any politics of multipartyism remaining in France. The fact that a large number of parties contest an election, with six of them major contenders, suggests that the nation is still fragmented in its politics and that there is still a lack of agreement on political fundamentals. Yet in 1962, for example, though a number of parties contested, and the largest of them won only about one-third of the votes, the electoral system produced a near majority for one contending party. It is difficult to see how this situation can continue without severe stresses on the whole political fabric. Not only is the electoral system restrictive in its denial of representation to the large number of smaller contenders, but it seems to punish the Communist party with unusual severity. In 1958, the party won about 19 percent of the first-ballot votes, yet it actually received only ten seats, as it became the victim of opposition in the run-off ballot. It fared somewhat better in 1962, winning 21 percent of the vote and 41 seats, while in 1967 it received 73 seats on 23 percent of the first-ballot votes. Nonetheless, although it is gradually approaching parity between seats and votes — suggesting that it is no longer the target of hostility for other components of the party system [26] — it is still short of even rough equality between seats and votes. (Perfect parity for the party in 1967, counting only first-ballot votes, would be 112 seats in the Assembly. The party remains second in first-ballot votes, third in number of seats in the Assembly.) It is one thing for small parties of a few electoral votes to be pummeled by the electoral system; it is quite another for one-fifth of the voters to be punished by an electoral system, especially in the light of the success of the new Federation of the Left, which received fewer first-ballot votes but many more seats. How long any political system can absorb the inevitable tension created by such apparent disenfranchisement is a question for which the Fifth Republic may yet provide an empirical answer.[27]

[26] The election of 1965 and the cooperation between components of the left in the legislative elections of 1967 will make much more difficult the exclusion of the Communist party from anti-Gaullist coalitions for the future. In the words of Philip Williams, "Once welcomed as allies, can the Communist worker or the Algerian refugee ever be pushed back behind the already crumbling walls of their political ghettoes?" "French Presidential Election of 1965," p. 28.

[27] In all fairness to the Fifth Republic and its institutions it must be noted that the Communist party, in its apparent new acceptability, may be able to participate on the left as a full partner in a new, very loose electoral coalition. However, such participation on any long-term basis is still very much hypothesis rather than fact.

The penalties paid by the Communist party are a direct result of the crucial feature of the second-ballot system, the coalescing between elections. Although the number of such instances is declining, the Communist candidates become the targets of other candidates who would rather see an enemy within the established pattern of party competition win the constituency than a Communist.[28] Particularly in 1958, the Communist candidate became the target for all parties whose candidates withdrew in favor of the one candidate who could beat the outcast. And that candidate was usually the supporter of General de Gaulle, especially in 1958 and 1962. The second-ballot system may present the voter with a dilemma. He may not wish the candidate opposing the Communist to win; but he may not wish the Communist to win either. In a large number of cases he faces a choice between either a Communist or a supporter of General de Gaulle, neither of whom he may feel represents his interests. The bargaining and maneuvering between first and second ballot may compound the injustice perpetuated by the single-member constituency to the point that representation occurs only in some formal sense to the voter denied any alternative remotely resembling his true desires. But, it has been said somewhere, nature abhors a vacuum, even if it be a political one. The aspect of the second-ballot system which creates such painful choices for the beleaguered voter may in fact — indeed in the case of France perhaps already has — create a course somewhat more acceptable to his tastes.

On the face of electoral data alone, it can be argued that the mechanism of the second ballot has created precisely that course. After the confusion of the legislative election of 1958, when some semblance of order began to be established, a suitable alternative for the French voter favoring neither de Gaulle nor the Communists may have begun to emerge within the

[28] Thus, even in the election of 1967 at least three Socialists refused the discipline of the federation of the left and refused to step down in favor of a Communist. See *Le Monde* (Paris), March 7–14, 1967, *passim*.

confines and the rules of the second ballot. Certainly, there seems ample evidence that in 1962 the voters were unhappy with their choices on either ballot. The number of voters declined, the number of blank or spoiled ballots increased, and the percentage of abstentions hovered around the 30 percent mark. Out of the very real dissatisfaction with the electoral choices available, a number of parties seemed to profit: the UNR increased its vote between first and second ballot, in a manner reminiscent of the 1958 election, while only two other parties, the Socialists and the Radicals, were in that happy position. Support for all other parties or groups declined between the first and the second ballot. In 1967, the tendency became more apparent. Between the first and the second ballot support increased for only two groups: the Fifth Republic group, generally supporting de Gaulle; and the Federation of the Left, generally the non-Communist left (although in 1967 it cooperated with the party on the second ballot). The second ballot, instituted partly to offset Communist strength and partly to give added representation to the loose Gaullist coalition of 1958, provided in the elections of 1962 and 1967 only mild punishment for the Communists on the first ballot and at the same time a chance for a relatively weak alternative, yet one more palatable than de Gaulle's supporters, to emerge. In 1967 on the first ballot the Federation won a single seat, while the Fifth Republic group won 68; on the second ballot the Federation won 115 seats, the Gaullists 176. Whether this pattern is a lasting one is not at issue here; what can be suggested is that in the absence of the second ballot, the Federation would not have become the force it now represents.

It is clearly the case that the electoral system did not by itself succeed in forcing a sharp centralization of the French political system. Between 1956 and 1962 there arose in the country a loose party based around de Gaulle which was able to attract a large following, in turn providing a parliamentary group larger than any single party provided by the Fourth Republic. Thus, parallel with, and perhaps preceding, the impact of a restrictive electoral system there was also a modernization and increasing cohesion in the entire French social

system that perhaps found its strength in the UNR.[29] Whatever the case, the electoral system has at least contributed to
legislative stability by arbitrarily inflating the representation
of the largest party and punishing smaller parties which had
been able to prevent stable majority government in the Fourth
Republic. That contribution, though real, has certainly been
a limited one, and the question remains whether the republic
has truly emerged into a new period of stability. Although the
UNR and its allies have held since 1962 a majority — occasionally shaky — in the National Assembly, the facts remain that
the UNR and its electoral coalition partners have gained no
more than about 35 percent of the first-ballot votes and that
the number of contending parties remains at ten or more. The
conjunction of a degree of homogeneity in the French social
system and a restrictive electoral system has produced a form
of stability, at the legislative level, but the extent of its pene-
tration into the fabric of French politics remains open to
question.

In fact, the second ballot is only a method of giving the
voter a form of preferential voting. It allows him to express
his primary allegiance on the first election and then on the
second ballot forces him to choose among a smaller number
of candidates who may have been among his lesser preferences.
The greatest difficulty with such a system lies in the two elections required for it to work: they are expensive, time-consum-
ing, and above all open the way for potentially undemocratic
maneuvering by the candidates. Other electoral systems have
been developed which allow multiple candidacies when two-
partyism seems difficult to achieve and a need exists to restrict
forcibly the number of serious competitors so that parliamentary majorities become possible. Such a system is the alternative vote, found most prominently in Australia.

[29] Perhaps underscoring the importance of the change in the electoral
system is the observation that France had begun to modernize long before de Gaulle. J. E. S. Hayward notes, for example, "It is generally
agreed, except by Gaullist apologists, that the foundations for French
economic success had been laid under the much maligned Fourth Republic." "Presidentialism and French Politics," *Parliamentary Affairs* 18
(Winter 1964/65), p. 25.

THE ALTERNATIVE VOTE: AUSTRALIA

The method of electing members to Australia's House of Representatives is a combination of the general principle of the single-member constituency with preferential voting. The device allows some flexibility of candidacies — to the extent that two members of the same party could conceivably run for the same seat — while it guarantees that eventually one candidate will achieve an absolute majority of the final electoral count. From the voter's point of view, the process is the same as that for a single transferable vote. The voter is presented with a ballot on which are listed all the candidates contesting for the single seat open in the constituency, and he merely ranks them in order of his preferences. The ballots are collected and counted, the preferences themselves are then totaled, and if any candidate receives a majority of the first preferences — that is, an absolute majority of the votes cast — he is declared elected. If there is no majority on the count of the first preferences, the candidate with the lowest number of first preferences is eliminated, the second preferences on those ballots are distributed, and any candidate who is able now to accumulate a majority is declared elected. If there is no majority on this count, then another is undertaken, and so on until there is one candidate with a majority of the votes cast, counting first, second, third, etc., preferences for this candidate all equally.

If electoral systems are the sole variable in party competition, the device used in Australia should result in a pattern similar to that of France, since there is the parallel to the second election in the counting of second preferences. The electorate should feel free to waste their minor party votes on their first preferences, knowing full well that if their own first preferences do not do well, their second preferences will be counted and will directly influence the final outcome of the election. But Australia has not developed a multiparty system parallel to that of the French Fifth Republic, and indeed in the majority of cases there has not been sufficient disagreement to force the counting of the preferences. The history of the alternative vote in Australia would seem to suggest that it is a refinement on the electoral system that is probably unnecessary, particularly in the light of the additional complexity that it forces upon the voter at election time.[30] It is a device primarily for the aid and comfort of minorities numerous and dissident enough to make normal majorities difficult to achieve and inadequate as representative devices. In Australia, this condition has not proved the case at all. Rather, the opposite has occurred as the single-member district elections have been decided far more often by majorities than by use of the preferential system.[31]

SUMMARY

The different electoral systems examined have all seemed to function as reasonably effective representative devices. In England, with its heritage of class conflict and enduring loyalties to mildly divisive issues there have been few elections without a substantial number of minority winners. Conversely, in the

[30] Indeed, the complexity of expressing preference combined with compulsory voting has produced an Australian phenomenon known as the "donkey voter," who marches to the polls, numbers his preferences from the top down, and then proceeds homeward. Presumably, the only anger shown by such a voter would be toward the compulsory aspect of voting, and his willingness to number from the top down (rather than from the bottom up, say) is an expression of some degree of satisfaction with the political system. See C. J. Masterman, "The Effect of the Donkey Vote on the Australian House of Representatives," *Australian Journal of Politics and History* 10 (August 1964), pp. 221–25. Cf. Henry M. Bain, *Ballot Position and Voter Choice* (Detroit: Wayne State University Press, 1957).

[31] The point is well made by Joan Rydon.

Multiple contests between 1910–51	50.03%
Total elections where preference was applied in order to determine the winner	22.69
Total elections in which preference system changed the result from first ballot	6.87

Thus, it is clear that (1) in only half the cases did more than two candidates contest the elections between 1910 and 1951; (2) that in about 77 percent of the elections the candidate got an absolute majority anyway; and (3) that only a small number of times was the final result any different from what would have been the case if the British simple plurality system had been used. See Joan Rydon, "Electoral Methods and the Australian Party System, 1910–1951," *Australian Journal of Politics and History* 2 (November 1956), p. 82.

more homogeneous society of Australia, there have been a very large number of majority winners under an electoral system seemingly designed more to encourage multipartyism than to produce parliamentary stability. Finally, the French system has only just produced a majority of one party in the legislature, and there exists in the political system a number of relatively even contenders.[32] Throughout all these cases, however, there has been a consistent theme: while the level of social cohesion and the degree of legislative division have varied from country to country, in each case the electoral system has created a parliament more consistent and more united than the society as a whole seems to be. Yet the electoral system has played a role whose value is debatable in democratic terms, for it has seemed to inflate the fortunes of larger parties while at the same time making life for the electoral opposition more difficult. Reconciliation of these two themes — the advantage of legislative stability and the injustice of distorted representation — is not a difficult task in a society that is relatively homogeneous and dominated by a generally shared consensus. But in states where consensus is elusive, where deep divisions are found in the general social system, plurality as an electoral technique has very severe disadvantages. For such societies a more representative technique is called for, and in answer to the call there is a plethora of contenders.

[32] Until 1968 there was no single party in the Fifth Republic able to claim a majority of its own members in the National Assembly. After the election of 1962, for example, there was a Gaullist majority but not one of the UNR.

CHAPTER IV

Proportional Representation

WHILE IT IS PROBABLY the fate of man forever to pursue the better gadget, the power of man as an inventor seems to have found its real focus in the electoral system, where his passion for politics is wed to his passion for gadgetry. Proportional representation and its various forms have become for a number of writers more than simply a means of electing officials to office for a reasonable period of power; it has become a problem of pure mathematics in which the goal is the closest approximation of the exact popular will at a given election time. Thus, straight proportionality of percentages has yielded to preferential voting, to cumulative voting, and so on. In some of the more complex systems the voter may have to list ten or more preferences on a rather formidable ballot, and then beleaguered election officials must spend many hours pursuing counts and recounts to find the final, mathematically exact winners. Through all of the complex proposing and theorizing, one goal is apparent: the equality of franchise, of equal and exact representation.

> The pure idea of democracy, according to its definition, is the government of the whole people, by the whole people, equally represented. Democracy, as commonly conceived and hitherto practiced, is the government of the whole people by a mere majority of the people exclusively represented. The former is synonymous with equality of all citizens; the latter, strangely

confounded with it, is a government of privilege in favor of the numerical majority, who alone possess practically any voice in the state. This is the inevitable consequence of the manner in which the votes are now taken, to the complete disenfranchisement of minorities.[1]

The words of John Stuart Mill stand as the clearest statement of the advocates of proportional representation for equal weight of citizen opinion. In service of this principle, no system is too complex, no technique incomprehensible.

If any modern democracy could rule itself directly, then there would be no problem. But size has corrupted the purity of original democracy, and until the day of some form of super and instant referendum, representation must substitute for continuous popular approval or rejection of policy for the mass state. To the proportional advocate the function of the electoral system is to produce a legislative assembly that most nearly approximates the patterns of thought and belief and emotion of the electorate at large, and any system that frustrates the replication of the electoral mood is a perversion of the principle of democratic representation. In the words generally attributed to Mirabeau,

> A representative body is to the nation what a chart is for the physical configuration of its soil; in all its parts, and as a whole, the representative body should at all times present a reduced picture of the people — their opinions, aspirations and wishes. . . .[2]

Thus, the function of the representative institution is reduced to absolute simplicity: apply to the problems and proposals of the day the desires of the electorate as though the representative institution were the electorate itself making the decision. In this way the democratic state can achieve through representation the popular assent unavailable because of the mechanical difficulties of direct popular participation in af-

[1] John Stuart Mill, *Considerations on Representative Government* (New York: Harper & Brothers, 1862), p. 145.

[2] Quoted in Donald J. Ziegler, *Prelude to Democracy: A Study of Proportional Representation and the Heritage of Weimar Germany, 1871–1920* (Lincoln: University of Nebraska, 1958), p. 4.

fairs of government. To the proportionalist, representative government cannot, and should not, serve any other function.[3]

The proportionalists are undoubtedly correct in assuming that one of the basic functions of a democracy is to open up the oligarchic elite in order that the policies of the state may benefit the population more widely. The destruction of the oligarchy is not pursued as an independent goal but is part of the desires of reformers to expand the role played by the general population in the affairs of its own state.[4] But the proportionalists would argue, of what value is the substitution of an oligarchy based on a majority for an oligarchy based on a mid-nineteenth-century concept of noblesse oblige? It is probably precisely the same minority that will be penalized in either case — the dissenters — and probably the hereditary oligarchy, if it has the slightest humanity in its veins, will be the more tolerant. Why should an electoral system be created in which a majority, perhaps only a very slim majority, is able to win and leave no representation for the minority at all? Why is it not possible to devise electoral systems which will give all parts of the electorate representation, in which there is no winner and only a very small number of losers in the contest for representation in the legislature? It is this concern with the failure of plurality systems to give minority representation in each constituency that motivates many of the advocates of proportional systems.

In the middle of the nineteenth century, when the general movement toward proportional representation seems to have

---

[3] It is beyond the space of this volume to list the various advocates of proportional representation. Suffice it to say that those who do not accept plurality as a legitimate device yet give even lip service to the problem of stability are the modern authors. See, for example, Enid Lakeman and James D. Lambert, *Voting in Democracies* (London: Faber & Faber, 1955), chap. 1; W. J. M. MacKenzie, *Free Elections* (London: George Allen & Unwin, 1958), chaps. 7 and 8. Both of these authors support the single transferable vote as the more effective form of proportional representation.

[4] Clarence Gilbert Hoag and George Hervey Hallett, *Proportional Representation* (New York: The Macmillan Co., 1926), pp. xii–xiii. "Hitch the voters to the 'representative' bodies right and their wills can exert a straight and effective pull for cleaner streets and streams, better schools and roads. . . ."

become serious, there was ground for concern. Suffrage was universally limited in the major powers, and those who could vote were not evenly represented. This was barely past the time of radical malapportionment, where in some districts electoral officers had to seek out the electors, so few were they; when weighted voting was common; and, as in the Prussian system, voting was done by classes rather than by equal suffrage. Not only was the apportionment of electoral equality inadequate, but the fluidity of party lines and the number of candidates might produce numbers of uncontested seats — thus giving those who disapproved not even the chance to express their disapproval — or seats where so many candidates contested that the winner might be the holder of only a small plurality of the votes cast in the election. The plurality form of election in England might easily yield a Parliament elected either by pluralities or no-contest majorities, from a limited suffrage, resulting in a parliamentary majority which could in no way be called representative. Reform of the system apparently required more than extension of the suffrage, for that would produce even greater disparities, as poor constituencies contained a great many electors and the rotten boroughs retained their sparse populations and controlled pluralities.[5]

The crusade of proportional representation developed against the seeming impossibility of constructive revision of legislative elections. Even if technical problems of suffrage and apportionment could be solved, any revision would leave the losers in constituencies unrepresented in the legislatures. To rescue this accumulated national minority without representation, the residues of support for countless numbers of losing candidacies throughout the nation, two basic plans emerged from the nineteenth century, one from Continental roots — perhaps Victor Considerant, scholar and sometime French mathematician — and the other from the pen of good English stock, that of Thomas Hare. The first system, called the list system after the form of the ballot given the voter, found its

---

[5] As indeed seemed the case in Imperial Germany as late as 1907. See George Dunlop Crothers, *The German Elections of 1907* (New York: Columbia University Press, 1941), p. 175.

greatest acceptance on the Continent and is to this day found usually in political systems that do not claim an English heritage. The Hare system, on the other hand, is found primarily in the areas of the world which have a connection with the Mother of Parliaments. In either case, whether list or Hare system, the main purpose is the same: the exact replication of the mood of the electorate at election time.

THE TWO BASIC FORMS
OF PROPORTIONAL REPRESENTATION

Both systems of proportional representation use the same basic technique to determine legislative seats: applying a quota to the total vote and awarding seats according to the number of quotas each party receives. In the purest form of each, the quota is calculated the same way, by merely taking the number of seats up for election, adding one to the number, and dividing it into the total vote. One is then added to that figure for the quota. Involved in this form of proportional representation is a fixed number of seats in the legislature, with the quota rising or falling as the total vote rises or falls. The most common variation of this system is setting a fixed quota and allowing the number of seats in the legislature to go up or down as the turnout increases or decreases election after election. In either case — the pure form or the major variation — the process is the same and the result is the same. For each quota that a contender receives, one seat in the legislature is awarded; no matter how small the vote of the contender or how large, only one quota is needed to earn one seat.

The major difference between the two systems lies in the nature of the contenders, what the voter sees, and what he supports when he votes. In the list system, the voter need not know the names of the candidates for whom he is voting, because the system is based exclusively on party and its list of candidates. Thus, the voter can only support a party, and in the original form of this system he cannot support any individual candidacies. When the voter enters the voting booth, he is presented with a series of parties, for one of which he can cast his vote. While the candidates of the party may be listed under the name of the party, it is not necessary for the act of voting that the voter know who the candidates are. Once all the ballots are cast, they are totaled, and each party receives the number of seats in the legislature corresponding to the number of quotas awarded it by the popular vote. Since more names are on the party lists than each party will win, the seats won are counted off beginning with the first name on the party list and proceeding down the list until all of that party's seats are assigned. Obviously, the further down the list an individual candidate's name lies, the less chance he has of getting elected, and the higher up on the list the better chance he has and probably the more important he is to the party. In any case, the party decides the position on the list, and there is no way that the voter can change that position to favor his particular hero.[6]

Any modifications of the pure list system obviously strike at two of the most important features of that system, its simplicity and the predominance of party. In fact, while the list system is ultimately simple as far as the voter is concerned — it works, of course, even with illiterates since the parties need only a symbol or color to identify their ballots — it does tend to isolate the voter from his government in an extraordinary manner. His only communication with the government is through the party, for there is no local constituency and there are in the pure system no local candidates of which the voter need be aware. Certainly, in the pure system of proportionality, the voter cannot express any direct feeling toward any candidate whatsoever, and thus must sense some form of isolation from the candidates and the general legislative system. Even the modification of the personal vote in Belgium or the

[6] A major attack against the Israeli list system stresses this point. See M. Z. Frank, "The Ben Gurion Battle," *New Leader* 49 (February 28, 1966), pp. 11–13. There are techniques employed in some systems — notably Belgium and Switzerland — which allow the voter to change ballot position, but such changes are often quite complicated to execute. See Christopher Hughes, *The Parliament of Switzerland* (London: The Hansard Society, 1962), pp. 37–40. Cf. U. W. Kitzinger, "The Belgian Electoral System," *Parliamentary Affairs* 16 (Spring 1963), pp. 155–57.

system of *panachage,* as cross-party voting in Switzerland is called, does not necessarily lessen the voter's plight. First, they obviously do not work for an illiterate or even semiliterate population. Secondly, they are rather complicated, and the obvious inclination of the less energetic voter is to vote the list ticket. In fact, if straight-ticket voting occurs in the United States, where elections seem largely candidate oriented, how likely is it that such modifications will be used in a system where party allegiance is the accepted tradition? [7] Finally, the personal vote is designed for use in exceptional cases rather than as a normal rule of voting, as in Belgium, where the exclusive use of the personal vote would usually render the same result as a list system. Add to this the fact that the list system usually uses either the whole nation or rather large multimember electoral districts, then the isolation of the voter remains only slightly ameliorated under these modifications.

The system proposed by Thomas Hare, using the single transferable vote, was apparently designed to bring candidacy home to the voter.[8] It is an extremely complex device, both for the voter and for the returning officer, but it does have the advantage of reducing party influence while maintaining the principle of proportionality. As in the list system, the constituencies must have a number of seats each, though the population of each district need not be as large as that for the list system for the proper functioning of the single transferable vote. A single list of candidates is presented to the voter, and the party affiliation of each candidate may or may not be included, since the workings of the system require only the name of the candidates and not their party. The voter ranks by number the candidates in order of his preference, with his most favored candidate being number one, his next number two, and so on down the list. If there are a couple of hundred candidates presumably he can rank them all if he chooses, although the functioning of the system is such that his effec-

[7] See, for example, Peter Campbell, *French Electoral Systems and Elections Since 1789* (Hamden, Conn.: Archon Books, 1965), p. 118.

[8] Thomas Hare, *The Election of Representatives,* 4th ed. (London: Longmans, Green, Reader, & Dyer, 1873).

tiveness usually ceases when his number of preferences exceeds the number of seats to be elected. The only function of party in the voter's activity is to guide him in his choice of preferences: if he wishes to cast all his preferences for one party, he can select those candidates, give them his top rankings, and go home.[9] Otherwise, he can ignore party guidelines entirely and merely indicate his preferences according to how he feels about each candidate on the list. This may become both difficult and impractical, however, as in the case where there are ten seats up for election and seven parties contesting; by rejecting party as a guideline, the voter faces the prospect of evaluating seventy candidates from which to select his ten top preferences.

Now the assignment of seats begins. First, a quota is established through some technique, the usual method being to divide the number of seats plus one into the total vote and add one to that figure. Any candidate who receives more than the quota is declared elected. Since this is a relatively rare occurrence, and probably suggests either the existence of an extremely popular candidate (such as Prime Minister) or an extreme concentration of support for one party, a second counting of the ballots is in order. The candidates are ranked in order of the number of the first-place preferences won, and the candidate with the smallest number of preferences is declared defeated. All the ballot papers which contained his name as the first preference are now separated out and added to the piles of the other candidates according to second preferences. Any candidate who now wins will have won by a combination of his own first preferences plus those second preferences assigned to him when the bottom candidate is removed from the running. If this distribution does not elect enough candidates to fill the seats up for election, then the new bottom man on the poll is removed and second preferences are distributed, a new count is undertaken, and the seats are assigned as candidates cross the quota threshold

[9] However, he must rank even his own party's candidates. Thus, if there were three seats up for election, he must rank his party's three candidates 1, 2, 3.

necessary to elect. This process continues through count after count until all the seats are filled. It may take one count or ten, but it must continue until all seats in the constituency have been filled. In Ireland the average number of counts in the election of 1957, according to one observer, was slightly more than five.[10]

Both the list and the Hare systems do satisfy the basic aim of the proportionalists. There are few wasted votes, and those are of the smaller parties not able to gain even close to the quota and probably not able to muster the strength to achieve representation under any electoral system. It is almost impossible for a large party to achieve an inordinate share of the legislature compared to its popular vote, for, while there are distortions in the final product, these distortions will not be nearly as great as they potentially could be under the plurality system used in Great Britain or the United States. Finally, there is a chance for the small party that might get far less than its "fair share" of the seats in the legislature to pull enough votes to get adequate legislative representation. Admittedly, there are some inequities in the two systems. Under the list system it is certainly possible for the total vote of the very small and unrepresented parties to be equal to several quotas, while the total vote of the candidates excluded under the Hare system might be equal to one or more quotas. Nonetheless, the systems do produce a level of proportionality simply impossible to attain under standard plurality systems.

THE EFFECTS OF THE LIST SYSTEM
ON PARTY COMPETITION

The best argument against list proportionality has been made with regard to Weimar Germany, and the specifics of that argument suggest that list proportional representation brought about the disintegration of the party system and the consequent inability of the legislature to act.[11] In the light of

---

[10] J. F. S. Ross, *The Irish Electoral System* (London: Pall Mall Press, 1959), p. 42.

[11] This point is important. If the remainder system had produced a large number of seats for small parties, or if the remainder system prevented any one party from winning a majority, it could rightly be con-

that argument, it is surprising to find that the number of parties actually successful in Weimar Germany during the 1920–28 period was about the same as the number before the First World War, although the number of potential contenders did increase. What is striking is the decline in the number of seats held by the most important parties: in 1912 two parties between them had an absolute majority of the Reichstag while they were the only parties to hold more than one-eighth of the seats; in 1920 five parties held more than one-eighth of the seats, indicating a substantial devaluation in strength of the major parties. Thus, in the change from the single-member district system of Imperial Germany to proportional representation under the Weimar regime there was no great multiplication of parties represented in the legislature but rather a gentle increase combined with a leveling out among parties in the system. More parties became important forces, fewer parties were major forces, and there was less opportunity for any one party to receive a majority of the legislature. The data on the Weimar electoral system suggest a model that is considerably different from that traditionally associated with proportional systems because in the Weimar case, while there were a vast number of competitors — forty-one in 1928 — there were relatively few successful parties and a rather small number of important parties. Thus, from 1920 through 1930 the number of parties gaining 10 percent or more of the Reichstag seats was five in 1920 and four in each election thereafter, almost exactly the same number of important parties (by the same criteria) in the Imperial Reichstag. In the case of Germany in the 1920s there is little question that a larger num-

---

demned. But the absence of anything close to a one-party majority in the Reichstag lessens the importance of the remainder system. The basic fact is that it was neither the remainder system nor really proportionality that produced a weak legislature; it was the failure of agreement in the society as a whole. As Arnold Brecht has noted, "It was essentially the diversified political composition of the German people rather than Proportional Representation which barred the way to strong democratic government." *Prelude to Silence* (New York: Oxford University Press, 1944), p. 131. See also Ziegler, *Prelude to Democracy*, pp. 82–83. For an opposing argument see F. A. Hermens, *Democracy or Anarchy?* (Notre Dame, Ind.: Review of Politics, 1941), chap. 10.

ber of parties contested the election but that the number of parties achieving representation did not substantially increase until 1928, and then only through the minor successes of a few small parties.

Not all list proportional systems share the characteristics of the Weimar system. Israel has employed the list proportional system, and one large party usually dominates the electoral scene with a plurality, but never a majority, of the seats in the Knesset; Argentina, on the other hand, changing from a sharp plurality system in 1962 to a list proportional one in 1963, moved to a position somewhere between the Weimar case of several intermediate parties and the Israel case of one large party and a number of smaller ones. In actuality, it is perhaps a totally new model that is called for, rather than the traditional one in which fractionalization is the immediate result of list proportionality. First, the introduction of a list system in both Argentina and Weimar Germany did not result in the immediate expansion of the number of successful parties as the traditional hypothesis might have suggested. The two major divisions that occurred — the split of the German Social Democrats and the breakup of the Argentine Radical Union — either took place before the introduction of list proportionality or for historical reasons not associated with the electoral system. Further, there seemed to be no general development of national minor parties, but rather small parties retained their regional bases and merely gained some ground in local representation. In at least two cases of list proportionality — contemporary Israel and Weimar Germany — and probably under any electoral system, the small parties would have won seats, whether the contest was single-member district, list proportionality, or something more exotic.[12] In any case, the immediate impact of the list system was not a multiplication in parties successfully gaining seats in the legislature.

A corollary to this first observation is the wider distribution that the list system seemed to bring among intermediate par-

[12] An argument admitted even by such an opponent of proportional representation as F. A. Hermens. See *Democracy or Anarchy?* esp. pp. 223–25.

ties. Although the number of minor parties did not change, the number of parties gaining significant membership in the legislature did change and seemingly at the expense of the major national parties. In two of the cases under consideration, Israel and Argentina, there was one major party able to capture about one-third of the seats in the legislature, while in Germany the best that the largest party was able to garner was about 23 percent of the seats. Thus, although there was no vast disintegration of the political party system, there was by no stretch of the imagination any centralization but rather a situation in which a dominant party was forced to seek aid from smaller parties to form the government. While the list system of proportional representation did make it impossible to attain anything like a majority party in the legislature, in all fairness it must be pointed out that in Argentina and Germany, both of which changed from forms of plurality system to proportional systems, parliamentary majorities had not been produced under recent use of plurality.

The second general conclusion leads from the first. The introduction of proportional representation did not result in the immediate expansion of the number of parties contending for office but did reflect the lack of social cohesion more than did the plurality systems that preceded proportional representation. In the two cases examined where a change in electoral systems took place, the legislature became more diverse while the percentage distribution of the popular vote remained about the same for the major parties. Thus, the advantage for the small contender under a list system is a guarantee of some form of representation but only at the expense of denying pluralities major control in the legislature. The inevitable tendency of plurality systems should, in the long run, be the forcing together of elements in the society, and if that fails at least plurality will give to the few large social groupings the power to run the state. It cannot be said that the list system — at least as it has been examined here — has that advantage. The list system of proportional representation has only the advantage of representing the social system as it stands; it provides neither stable legislative majorities — albeit majorities based on pluralities — nor any pressures toward political integration which might precede increased social cohesion. List proportionality tends to stress social disunity; plurality tends to mask it.

PROBLEMS OF LIST PROPORTIONAL REPRESENTATION

While the list system performs admirably the basic purpose of proportional representation, it has a number of features which are not easily accepted by the modern democrat and which tend to dilute the beneficial aspects. There is, first, the obvious role of the party, which can almost dictate the election of party functionaries by placing them high on the ballot and conversely punish the irritating but perhaps necessary member by placing him far down the ballot, safely out of electoral reach except in the most impressive landslide victories. Because the party has the power to reward or punish by the rank on the list ballot, it in effect has the power to restrict the role of the legislator to the whims of the party leadership and the party machinery, forcing an ideological consistency which might indeed deprive the legislator of the freedom of action to which he might feel entitled. In this sense, then, the party has the power of rewarding or punishing, of partially dictating attitudes of the candidate — all roles usually assigned to the electorate as a whole rather than to a party bureaucracy or conference. In a pure list legislature it is reasonable to argue that the electorate may decide the fate of a few of the members but that the vast majority of the legislature is the product of party manipulation and party favoritism. This particularly would seem to be true in the case of the well-established major party with a reasonably large and stable following in the electorate.

The second criticism of the list system is the insertion of party between the voter and his representative. The elector cannot express his displeasure through any means but refusing to vote for the party, which seems something of a drastic move, if only one of his favorites is placed down the list in harm's way. The list system furnishes him with no recourse other than acceptance of the list as it stands at election time, with the hope that displeasure can be expressed through other party channels. Of course, the voter can attempt to influence the party conference in the direction of his favorite, but since party congresses tend to represent the workers in the vineyards of party wars rather than the mere voting membership of the party, this is a strategy of doubtful effectiveness. Obviously, he has no recourse to the representatives because they are not district representatives; they are all members from multimember districts, and they do not owe their election to the voter so much as they owe their success to their party's willingness to place them high up on the ballot. While it is certainly in the representative's self-interest to go along with the party rather than with the particularism of blocs of individual voters, it must be small solace to the voter to know that his representative has more of any eye to the party as a whole than to any member of his own district.[13]

It is perhaps the all-or-nothing feature of list systems that seems to make them suspicious electoral devices. The voter must take all of the party doings, or none of them, and the same applies to the party's candidates. Most list systems ask the voter to accept all the party candidates for a large number of seats, usually in electoral districts so large that any voter unhappiness is poorly expressed. In a single-member district system, there is the relative closeness of candidate and voter; potentially, there are also independent candidates. But under list proportionality by the very act of voting for the party the voter endorses all that the party has done and will do, since he has no way of indicating lukewarm acceptance through either the nomination process or by splitting his vote among

[13] The difficulties presented by list proportionality are frequent objects of criticism. In the most hostile attack against proportional representation in general and list proportional representation in particular, F. A. Hermens mentions party control as antidemocratic and destructive of the internal democracy of the parties. *Democracy or Anarchy?* pp. 231 ff. Most of these same criticisms are applied to the Israel Knesset in Benjamin Akzin, "Israel Knesset," in the *Israel Yearbook 1967* (Tel-Aviv: Israel Yearbook Publications, Ltd., 1967), p. 76. Even the defenders of proportional representation acknowledge these difficulties. Cf. Lakeman and Lambert, *Voting in Democracies,* p. 199.

several parties. Thus, the list system may reflect quite accurately how extensive support for the party is in the general society, but there is no method of determining how intensive that support is for a selected candidate or in a small segment of the society.[14] The mandate of a party in a list system may appear to be support for a program or ideology but the separation from the voter, the dominance of party machinery, and the impersonality of the party ballot all suggest that the exact nature of this representation is somewhat suspect.

Various methods of preference have been introduced from time to time in order to ameliorate some of these vices. List systems incorporating these modifications add perhaps needless complications to the act of voting when there is available the Hare system — proportional representation by preference alone — which satisfies all of these arguments while seeming to maintain the general principle of proportionality. Indeed with the single transferable vote the party may dictate its nominees if it so desires but disappointed members may campaign as independent candidates if they so desire.[15] If the general pattern of nominations is approved by the electorate as a whole, with one or two exceptions in the list, voters can mark their preferences for those candidates of the party which are preferred and then punish the party for not nominating more acceptable candidates for the remainder of the seats. Thus, the electorate retains control over the winning party and the losing party, and over which members of the winning party will win and which will lose. In a close constituency, in fact, the defection of a relatively small number of voters from some candidates of the major party to one or two independent dissenters may make the difference between a clean sweep by one party and the post-election knowledge that a slightly

[14] Benjamin Akzin, "Israel Knesset," p. 79, mentions that as many as 50 percent of Israel's parliament, elected under the list system on a national constituency, live in Tel-Aviv, leaving a large part of the country underrepresented in any but a formal sense.

[15] However, the existence of independent candidates under plurality would seem to be more effective than under the Hare system, since independents could more easily blackmail regular party candidates than under proportional representation.

more attentive party organization could have prevented the election of independents. The merits of the single transferable vote are obvious, but how well it works out in practice is another question.

THE HARE SYSTEM AND
PARTY COMPETITION

On first examination the single transferable vote is a formidable contender as the most equitable of electoral systems. It is able, precisely because of its transferable feature, to prevent the nomination of party hacks. Voters may choose as they will from the list of candidates and need not support any single one they feel is not worthy, regardless of the party that supports him; for example, in a normal election in Ireland, about 15 percent of the vote usually goes to nonparty, or group, candidates. The Hare system penalizes small nationally distributed parties who are unable to muster enough votes in a limited constituency to meet any single quota, and their votes are consequently discarded. Thus, in a nine-seat constituency, the quota will be 10 percent of the vote cast plus one, and most minor parties should be able to achieve at least that threshold or their cause could not be very popular; but in a three-seat constituency, where the quota is 25 percent of the vote plus one, the problem of obtaining a quota is more formidable, and as a consequence in the smaller districts the larger parties tend to be overrepresented. Finally, the Hare system gives the voter a name, a clear identification for which he must cast his ballot, and that relationship may go a long way toward overcoming the potential estrangement between man and his government. Given all these advantages, it is not difficult to understand the passionate attachment of some to the technique.

The Hare system also has many disadvantages.[16] First, it does not always yield a proportional result, particularly in smaller districts. Most embarrassing for the proportional rep-

[16] Cornelius O'Leary, *The Irish Republic and Its Experiment with Proportional Representation* (Notre Dame, Ind.: University of Notre Dame Press, 1961), pp. 50–52. The following analysis is based largely on O'Leary.

resentation advocate is the Irish election of 1957 in which the party Fianna Fail won a majority of seats in the Irish Parliament, the Dail, while winning only a plurality of the popular vote. In fact, a brief examination of the results of the sixteen elections between 1923 and 1957 suggests that the largest party almost always benefits from some distortion in the electoral results, on the average of about five seats an election. The distortion may be explained in a number of ways. First, in any multimember district where one party is in a large majority, it can win all the seats with less than all the votes. In Ireland, with a great number of three-seat constituencies, the major parties can win two of the three seats by simply acquiring half the votes, two quotas of the necessary three. Secondly, the smaller the constituency the larger the proportional quota needed to elect, and the larger the total vote acquired by small parties over the whole country; but this vote is insufficient in any one constituency to meet one quota. Thus, the small constituency, which seems necessary for the close relationship of representative to elector, may also breed distortion in the results and leave a large percentage of the voters without representation.[17]

Viewing the Hare system in a more complex political system than that of Ireland raises even clearer doubts about its advantages.[18] In New York, specifically in the 1937 city council election, the single transferable vote encouraged multiple

[17] A related difficulty is inherent in any district system, whether Hare or plurality. It is simply impossible to draw district lines in such a way that population is distributed evenly among the districts. In Ireland, for example, the districts may not vary more than 10,000 per representative, that is, no fewer than 20,000 population nor more than 30,000 per seat. Obviously, if smaller districts are coincident with one interest and larger with another, competing interest, some meaningful distortion may occur. The problem has recently been adjudicated. See "Popular Representation in the Irish Parliament," *Bulletin of the International Commission of Jurists*, no. 20 (September 1964), pp. 46–48.

[18] For illustrative purposes only the borough of Brooklyn is used, although similar patterns occurred in all city boroughs. The source of the data is the *Annual Report of the Board of Elections in the City of New York for the Year 1937*, prepared by Edward J. McGowan, Chief Clerk (New York, 1938). The complete tabulation for each candidate for all counts is found following p. 46.

candidacy to the point that veritable bedsheet ballots were produced, with battalions of names competing for a relatively small number of seats. In the borough of Brooklyn alone, ninety-nine candidates competed for nine seats, requiring sixty counts of the ballots and three weeks to declare the final elected candidates. Even so, it might be argued that such an electoral system is more just, if not more expeditious, than any other. The obviously unsuccessful candidates who received few first preferences were eliminated on the first or second count, and their votes were transferred over to other candidates. If a voter's first and second choices are eliminated, perhaps his third or fourth (or even his ninety-ninth) will serve one candidate and push him over the top. Two problems, however, arise to plague this reasonable contention. First, a number of voters will simply not list preferences that far, and thus the votes that they cast, which may accumulate to a sizable number, will be effectively eliminated. In the borough of Brooklyn in 1937 this figure was about 150,000 or about 21 percent of the vote cast. Secondly, the assumption that the voter's fifth preference is as valid as his first — or even valid by the same criteria as his first — is open to serious doubt. Obviously, a first choice is a first choice and not a second choice. Further, even if the voter casts all his preferences for only the candidates of one party, the actual workings of preference may deny him the pleasure of seeing his first choice elected (presumably given to one candidate for other than capricious reasoning) while a fifth choice of that party may be supported sufficiently by a large enough random group to push him over the top. An election system so long and involved, while at the same time so easily distorting the intent of voters, may seriously weaken the bonds of voter and elected.

The experience in New York, or at least in Brooklyn, with the single transferable vote seems to exhibit all of the weaknesses of the Hare system with none of the strengths. One party won a majority of the seats from Brooklyn without even close to a majority of the first preferences, six of the nine successful candidates received less than the quota, and more than a fifth of the valid ballots were exhausted in their preferences by the end of the counting — all suggesting that the Hare system did not function well in its New York application. Perhaps as disturbing as these problems was the delay in producing the electoral result. Because the number of counts in Brooklyn was so large, the electorate and the machinery of government waited three weeks before learning who were to be the City Council representatives from the borough, the largest of five city boroughs. Although the single transferable vote proved only slightly more equitable than the single-member district system used later for elections to the council, it greatly complicated the normally serene and controlled political atmosphere of New York.

It is perhaps simple to say that the major problems faced in New York City were caused by mass unfamiliarity with the new electoral system and that time would have given the transferable vote more of a chance than it had in its brief ten years. Certainly it has worked in Tasmanian state elections, Ireland, and a number of American cities; [19] but these are small, reasonably compact, entities, and all together their total vote is perhaps not significantly larger than that of New York City alone. They all have the additional advantage of small districts, or are small enough themselves in size so that the basic electoral unit is sufficiently homogeneous to prevent a mass splitting of the popular vote, as occurred in New York of 1937. Ireland and Tasmania had at the inception of their political systems enough forces pressing for homogeneity to make almost any system operable as an electoral device. There were logical and reasonably positive bases for party attachment around great issues, and this contributed to the stability of party activity. The outstanding characteristic of New York during the Depression was reform, but reform conceived negatively against the Democrats, during a period of social dislocation of some magnitude. Thus, it can be argued that the necessary social homogeneity was absent from the New York political system, and proportional representation in the form of the Hare system never really had a chance.

[19] See, for example, Ralph A. Straetz, *PR Politics in Cincinnati* (New York: New York University Press, 1958).

A number of preconditions is essential for the single transferable vote to work effectively and efficiently. Size of the electoral district is important, as is sufficient social homogeneity to force the political system together so that the incidence of independent candidacies or splinter parties without intense regional support is kept to a minimum. The requirements of proportionality are partially satisfied if these preconditions are met, but some of the equitable benefits of proportional representation are denied by the existence of these factors. Distortion occurs, and at the same time the electorate is asked to participate in a system that is complicated both for the electoral official and for the voter. In short, the simplicity of the list system is exchanged for questionable stability and perhaps less equitable representation. The advantage of the Hare system over the list system, then, must be judged solely in terms of party, for in the Hare system the effective control of party machinery is gone and is replaced by the will of the electorate. But comparison can be made with single-member plurality systems, in which the nominating process is controlled by the electorate through the device of the primary or, failing that, through the obvious possibility of independent candidacies at election time. Caught between the Scylla of injustice and Charybdis of complexity, the single transferable vote would seem to have the dubious distinction of being consumed simultaneously by both.

A GENERAL ANALYSIS OF
PROPORTIONAL REPRESENTATION

In the search for electoral justice the ingenuity of man has created and the state has employed devices of number and complexity to boggle the mind. Electoral machinery has been applied which uses percentages and proportions, and even rankings by voter preferences, in order to achieve more equitable representation of social groups in the modern democratic state. Occasionally, these systems have seemed to pursue the goal of mathematical equality at the expense of the voter's capacity to comprehend the act of voting and the electoral official's ability to produce clear, unequivocable results in a reasonable period of time. The pursuit of mathematical equality has not only produced strains upon institutions by denying them stable majorities with unified goals for governmental activity but has also imperiled the electorate's understanding of the workings of the system. If the electoral system threatens the psychological linkage between governed and governor, through complexity in the act of voting or in the certification of results, mathematical equality may be achieved at the very high cost of voter alienation.

It seems true beyond question that systems of proportional representation reduce markedly the ability of any one party to achieve a majority in the legislature. In any system of proportional representation the emphasis is on legislative replication of social groupings, and inherently this will mean in any but the most cohesive state the representation of more than two parties. The additional groups may be a number of well-organized and disciplined parties or may simply be a cluster of independents, but the effect of proportional systems seems largely to force coalition government upon the state, whether it be coalition government of a large party in league with small parties or independents, or a coalition composed of a group of intermediate parties whose strength is roughly all equal. Fractionalization of the legislative party system will take different forms depending upon the system of proportionality used. On the one hand, pure list systems without restrictions on the number or size of parties favor small parties whose district strength may be negligible but whose national strength is sufficient to win a seat or two in the legislature. In any close legislative division, these parties may be able to decide the fate of governments and place demands perhaps far outweighing their true strength in the nation. On the other hand, different proportional systems tend slightly to favor larger parties by using small districts in conjunction with such techniques as the single transferable vote. In either case, the normal pattern results in a government by coalition and a legislature without one clear party voice.

Coalitions do form and occasionally do manage to govern well. Perhaps the greater problem presented by proportional representation is not the instability which it produces among government majorities but the failure to produce an opposition with a distinct political nucleus. Even if a majority party forms in the legislature and is able to form a government stable enough to pursue a coherent program, the disintegration of the opposition may in the long run be as harmful as the absence of an initial legislative majority. It is true that the outparties in cooperation with defectors from government ranks may form a negative majority capable of ousting the government of the day, but the function of opposition in the democratic state is more than destruction of the government majority. It is also the capacity to present a critique of governmental programs and to provide the voter with a feasible second choice for government of his country. It is here that the baneful effects of multipartyism are most severely felt. Even if the government is not based on a majority party in the legislature, it is most likely to comprise the largest party in the assembly in concert with just enough additional support to make up a majority. The important role of opposition is left to the remainder, a group of parties unable to agree sufficiently among themselves at election time to provide electoral coalitions, which now must systematically criticize governmental actions. Since they were unable in the election to present a united front, it is doubtful if in the assembly they will be able to present one critical voice and one set of programs that will be recognized by the voter as a viable alternative. An electoral system which fails to provide either a single stable majority to support the government or a partially united opposition to act as a constant alternative does not seem to serve parliamentary democracy with great efficiency.

By the manipulation of quotas or the use of small districts, most systems of proportional representation attempt to reduce the disintegrative effects of the proportional election through the application of restrictive devices. Whether it be a requirement that a party must receive a certain percentage of the popular vote to receive any seats (as in the case of Israel where a party must receive 1 percent of the total vote regardless of how many quotas it may earn) or whether it be a requirement that a party must receive more than one quota in any given multimember district to receive any representation at all, there is usually some device to prevent the disintegration of legislative representation into a vast number of very small party delegations. In those systems which do not use a national constituency but rather a number of subnational multimember districts, the effect is usually to provide punishment for only a certain kind of minority, evenly spread across the nation, and actually to reward the intense regional minority able to garner sufficient strength in a limited number of districts to evade the restrictive features. A combination of decentralized districts and other restrictive features produces a variety of represented groups. First, the major national parties with more than enough votes to surpass any restrictive device will obviously be represented in the assembly and will provide the vast bulk of the membership. The second category of parties represented will be parties which have strong regional ties in the electorate. While its national strength may be limited, the regional strength of such a party may make it the most potent political force in a small area; and as a regional party with a narrow focus of ideas, it is not only a potentially disruptive element in any legislature but also a potential centrifugal force in the society. It is, of course, unfair to suggest that a regional party may prosper unduly only under proportional representation. Obviously, its intense local following will allow it representation under a single-member district system as well. Because proportional representation maximizes the possibility of a heterogeneous legislature and a single large party usually needs additional support to form a coalition government, the regional party may be able to assume an importance far greater than its actual strength in the nation would warrant. While restrictive features of most proportional representation systems do benefit the larger and more important political contenders, they also open the doors to smaller, and perhaps dysfunctional, political units.

The argument against proportional representation in mass democracy is usually phrased in functional terms, such as multipartyism, distortions, parliamentary instability, and so on.[20] Indeed, all the criticisms that are applied to proportional representation would seem to indicate its lack of coherence with parliamentary systems. Other criticisms can be put forward that are equally important. There are fundamental assumptions that proportionalists must make about the nature of representation and the legislative role, and although these assumptions are far more difficult to discuss than the functional difficulties of proportional representation, they are nonetheless crucial to its operation. To these more general considerations some attention should now be given.

The modern legislature exists in a time of executive orientation. Not only is the world of the developed nations one that demands swift response to nuclear threat, but the problems of emergence from dark pasts has forced upon emergent nations the necessity of sure decisions without undue disagreement. Further, the nature of these decisions — technical, economic, or social decisions usually beyond the ken of the average elector — demand the constant attention of technical experts, highly trained in esoteric arts of planning strategy and social engineering, who usually are found in the executive. Thus, the days of the innovative legislature seem past, and the future seems to demand a legislature which can exercise a determined and systematic check over the power of a technically competent administrative organization. Thus — and this seems increasingly true in developed regimes — the modern legislature becomes partly the counterweight to the preponderant executive as often as it is the innovating and systematic creator of policy. A legislature constantly at war with itself makes a poor participant in such a contest.

Whether this twentieth-century view of the legislature or its more traditional counterparts is adopted, the legislature becomes an institution with a life separate from its constituencies. The role of the legislature is not passive, nor is it a restricted one of merely transmitting moods and attitudes to the policy-making process. Rather, the function of the legislature — of both the majority and opposition within it — is to

[20] Criticisms specifically refuted in volumes such as Lakeman and Lambert, *Voting in Democracies,* esp. chap. 8.

attempt as best it can to act between elections for the best interest of the body politic. Its task would be simplified if there were constant referenda on every subject before the legislature. But this is not the case, and, in fact, most of the issues on which a legislature acts would not excite the passions or political fever of many of its constituents. The legislature must decide the best it can according to its information and political experience. In short, even if at election time the legislature is indeed Mirabeau's mirror image of society — and that is perhaps open to question — there is strong doubt that the legislature can maintain this mirror image once the election is over. First, issues and conditions change, and it is impossible to argue that inaction must prevail because there has been no election under the changed circumstances. Secondly, what may have seemed a reasonable position for a party to assume on the hustings may not be so reasonable under strong light of official testimony and hard scrutiny in legislative committees. Finally, it may be only the legislature which is able to divert a demagogic executive from a potentially popular, but dangerous, path; and thus it may be the legislature which is called upon to pull back from the brink an executive bent on destruction. The legislature must assume a role somewhat independent of the constituencies which have elected it; it must become an institution with a life of its own and not merely a gathering of ambassadors reacting to the slightest constituency whim.

At this point the nature of a proportionally elected representative body becomes important. A legislature designed to be less a governing body than an arena for the confrontation of quarreling elements in the society — albeit elements justly represented — may be unable to fulfill the role of a vigorous institution united behind a set of purposes to defend or a set of proposals to implement. Behind the general theories of proportional representation there is an assumption about the nature of the legislative process and the role of the legislature in the general political process. The legislature is thought of as the clearing house for conflicts in the society rather than as an active, innovating institution in the workings of the political system. Because it is not assumed that the legislature need act as a unit, there is no felt necessity for the electoral system to produce anything but a divided reflection of tensions within the society. The advocate of proportional systems of representation need only be concerned with the attainment of an exact mathematical representation in the legislature and not with a lack of stability in the political process. For the proportionalists the legislature is a channel of communication between represented and governors, and it is not in itself an institution of government. It is thus merely a creature and extension of the electoral process.

The assumptions of the proportionalist give rise to a second, related problem: the limited definition of representation. In the general theories of proportional representation, the electorate is seen in group terms, linking arms across county and regional lines until they make up one quota. The supporters of a successful candidate have nothing in common but their desire to elect an individual who stands for a limited set of goals but who has little personal attachment to the voters who elected him. Thus, the voters create what Walter Bagehot calls the voluntary constituency, forming together amorphously behind one candidate and then disappearing until the next election.[21] One feature of the multimember constituency is the distance between the elector and his representative. If a voter is assigned by law to one constituency, which has one representative, there is a specific and tangible relation between the voter and the representative. If the representative is only one of several from a large constituency, particularly if he is an independent, one-of-a-kind elected along with a number of party regulars from the same constituency, there is little to link him to the constituency once he is in office. He was not elected by a majority, nor was he usually elected by a sizable minority. His constituency — the voters who came together to elect him — has disappeared into the much larger confines of the general electorate, and in a very real sense his constituency has disappeared as rapidly as it formed. He must, however,

[21] Walter Bagehot, *The English Constitution* (Ithaca, N.Y.: Cornell University Press, 1966), pp. 166–68.

still make his decisions as a voting member of the legislature. He has little guidance from his constituency, since it is impossible for him to discover from what part of the large multimember constituency his support came. The member's only alternative is either to fall back upon his party, if any, for guidance, or to assume that his ideological positions were the deciding factor in his success. In either case, his cues for legislative decision must come from some source not directly connected to the whole constituency which elected him.

The difficulties such a member presents to a legislature are particularly acute when the member is of a sharp ideological bent. In that case he knows generally what variety of voter supported him, one that could not under a more limiting system usually gain representation. It does not advance his political ambitions to serve the whole constituency, because its members are unnecessary to his success. He only need act in such a way that, first, his voluntary constituency, wherever they are, may know that he is following his commitments, and secondly, that they will remain cohesive in any election in the near future. His role cannot then be one of moderation, but it must be one that is distinct and in a real sense dysfunctional, lest he be swallowed by the general pattern of politics in the nation. It is true that under any system of election there will be such members — one cannot help but think of certain members of the American Congress who come from markedly ethnic districts in northern urban areas — but the chances that such a candidate will get a large enough plurality to win in a single-member district system are far less than in a multimember proportional system. Proportional systems open the way for such members of legislatures, while plurality systems tend to reduce their incidence and increase the chances for a more moderate legislature.[22]

22 The comment by Maurice Duverger is pertinent here: "The manifest result of the majority vote with a single ballot, with its tendency to foster the two-party system, is to cut out the secondary divisions of opinion, crystallizing public feeling around two main competing trends; while proportional representation fosters the proliferation of shades of opinion by allowing each to set up its own party." "The Influence of Electoral Systems on Political Life," *International Social Science Bulletin* 3 (Summer

Electoral systems based on the principle of proportional representation exact a high price in exchange for mathematically precise representation. The first casualty is usually the possibility of majority party government. The role of the party is vastly increased — in some systems more than in others — and the interests of the whole constituency must usually take a back seat to some larger focus. In addition, the possibility of immoderate dysfunctional elements increases markedly, especially among systems utilizing a large number of multimember constituencies. In any electoral system which can produce a normal legislative majority, the influence of these elements is restricted by the presence of stable majorities or major parties, but in an electoral system designed to represent diversity rather than produce stability, the influence of divergent representatives is enhanced. Finally, proportional representation in practice usually sees the electorate solely as electoral groupings and not as members of a constituency in which a majority must constantly be fashioned. Whether in the long run a legislature can operate apart from the interests of the individual voters without sacrificing confidence in the political system is a difficult question. But the very possibility raises new doubts about the utility of proportional systems in large and developed political systems.

1951), p. 334. This analysis is correct as long as there is an absence of crystallization in the political system. Cf. S. S. Nilson, "Social Condition and Electoral Systems," *ibid.*, p. 360. See also the discussion of the crystallized politics of South Africa in this volume, Chapter 3.

CHAPTER V

Elections and National Integration

ALL NATIONS in which popular elections are held begin with a problem and end with an advantage. The problem is the existence of dissident groups which must be brought into national political life, whose demands must be met consistent with national goals. All national political systems must have some techniques for coalition building, whether they be ideological, symbolic, or political. It is through concession to the demands of potentially hostile groups or regions that a successful coalition is built, while these same concessions reduce the centrifugal forces pulling the society apart. The need to form a successful electoral coalition that will produce an effective legislative party organization is an integrating device for the system as a whole and for parts of the society that might not normally feel they have a stake in the government.

The advantage that the state derives from popular elections comes from the act of voting. By the very act of casting his ballot, the citizen of the state is involved in a way that alienated or uninvolved voters are not. The casting of a ballot is an affirmation of the effectiveness of representative government, for if that were not the case, those in opposition to the existing government would have little incentive to vote. Casting a ballot is more than a choice between parties. It is the direct involvement of the individual in the political system, in the process of government; and for any state — particularly one in the beginning stages of development — that is a very important achievement.

Elections are more than just the occasional activation of a political institution. They appear to be social institutions, strange ones at that, because through the electoral system individuals in the political system respond to the whole — the electors respond to the decisions past, present, and potential of the government that is attempting to serve their interests. An understanding of this process is made more complex by the myriad possible alternatives open to, and motivations of, the voters and the implications of those motivations. A particularly complicating factor is the nonvoter. He may be relatively satisfied with the political patterns of the past, see no reason for these patterns to change, and so place politics relatively low on his scale of priorities. He is totally integrated into the political system, for his goals and desires are in his eyes identical with the policy patterns of the prevailing government, and those attitudes are shared by the mass population. But the nonvoter may also not participate because he perceives the utter impossibility of any of his ilk winning office under the prevailing system. He is not domestic and tranquil, but alienated and unhappy and far from integrated into the prevailing political system. Although politics may be very high on his scale of priorities, the act of voting is meaningless precisely because the political system has not produced, for whatever reason, his kind of party or candidate, and his only rational course of action is to withhold his support from the political system. His participation in the affairs of state is limited to fulminations and railings against his own political regime.[1]

ELECTORAL SYSTEMS AND DISSIDENTS

At the juncture of ideological dissidence, voter alienation, and elections lies a good deal of debate. In its crudest form

[1] Perhaps this voter is found in such movements as the Poujadiste in France of 1956. See, for example, Howard Lewis Rosenthal, "Contemporary French Politics and Sub-Strata Analysis" (Ph.D. diss., M.I.T., 1964), pp. 129 ff.

one side of the argument runs something along these lines: Proportional representation, because it encourages the development of third parties, encourages dissidence through ideological parties and leads inevitably to confused and unhappy politics. The other side of the debate should run something like this: Plurality systems, characterized by single-member districts that reward local pluralities, penalize minorities severely, leaving them without a shred of representation unless they can muster sufficient strength to defeat any coalition against them, and thus contribute directly to alienation and estrangement from politics. While both of these arguments contain elements of reality, both are in part caricatures of much more complex processes. In some systems of proportional representation there are few, if any, activists who could be called truly ideologically dissenting, while in some plurality systems there is history of ideological movements — even in the staid and secure electoral system of the United States there have been recent rumblings of ideology.

It seems obvious that dissident ideological movements that lack the ability and the will to combine with more pragmatic parties face a better future in proportional systems than they do in most plurality systems. Adopting a threefold set of rewards — material, solidary, and ideological [2] — one can easily suggest why the proportional system is the better home. All three rewards are present in the proportional systems, while there is a very good chance that only two will be present in plurality systems. The fact that third parties do not do well electorally in the United States, for example, suggests that material rewards for the party faithful are limited. And to the voter, who knows full well that the cards are stacked against his party, the unyielding support of a losing cause year after year is a noble, uplifting, yet futile endeavor. The logic that leads to such a depressing conclusion for those who do not share in the happy consensus that regularly dominates most plurality systems is fallacious, and on at least three counts. First, there is the obviously embarrassing notion that

[2] The schema employed by Peter Blau in *Exchange and Power in Social Life* (New York: John Wiley & Sons, 1964), p. 238.

by emphasizing the stability of governing bodies through the process of conflict resolution prior to the legislative stage, plurality systems may produce by the process of exclusion from policy making the very ideological parties of dissent that supposedly plague proportional representation. Second, the plurality system is peculiarly vulnerable to regional concentrations of voters (where a properly distributed 51 percent can win 100 percent of the seats), and there is no rule that says that dissident ideological movements must necessarily be randomly distributed. Finally, within either form of electoral system a faction not able to win on its own as a third party may move into the organization of an established party and subvert it to its own ends, vastly amplifying its own power by attachment to traditional voters of that party. The case of the 1964 Republicans is only one example.

This last observation is one which merits further examination. Takeover is encouraged vastly by the plurality system, for the very simple reason that traditional voters of that party's persuasion are faced with voting for their own party, who has nominated some rather peculiar candidate, or casting their ballot for the devil (the other party) and selling their birthright. While many may stay home, many more will most likely cast their ballots for the peculiar candidate rather than for Beelzebub. An internal coup in the party is enormously aided, then, by the traditional commitment of voters to that party and against the other. But, ironically, aid also comes insofar as political integration, supposedly characteristic of plurality systems, has reduced the political interest of the tranquil voter. Extremist politics may also be a function, in short, of the lack of interest in the majority of voters in their own political system's on-going character.[3] If organizational activities are left to a few who have the interest to participate, these few moderates may be overwhelmed by internal subversion on the part of the highly politicized, yet

---

[3] Implicit in the argument that Senator Barry Goldwater won the 1964 Republican nomination by taking precinct battles in the early sixties by default. The argument in the text is merely another variation of the observations of Robert Dahl in *Preface to Democratic Theory* (Chicago: University of Chicago Press, 1956), chap. 6.

alienated, faction of the party which moves into organization and comes to dominate party machinery. In that particular case the moderating tendencies of the plurality system may become instead a force toward an immoderate politics, since the only alternatives to the moderates are to remain in the party, remain home, or to aid the other party, the traditional enemy. Starting a third party will only ensure the victory of the enemy party and inflict few, if any, casualties on the ideological movement, whose solace may be in ideological reward more than material incentive anyway.

When viewed from these perspectives, the neat argument that plurality systems encourage moderate politics becomes less absolute. Rather, it may be said in the long run that plurality systems are freer from dissident ideological movements than proportional systems because the political system was moderate enough in its inception to tolerate the forced integration characteristic of most plurality electoral systems. To this observation must be added a second: while it is not always the case that plurality electoral systems are barriers to ideological dissidents, such electoral devices do place obstacles in their way and do tend to create unhappy minorities who are unable to attain victory. To that extent, plurality systems may furnish the fuel for ideological fires, they may encourage dissident voters looking for some other alternative, and they may provide the groundwork for a more explosive dissent when it finally comes. At least proportional systems allow the ideological parties the right of representation and deny them the charge that they have been left out in the electoral cold while they have accumulated a substantial electoral vote. The ease by which representation is attained under proportional systems may contribute to stability and integration in the sense of a safety valve, while the difficulty of attaining representation for a new movement under plurality may provide the opposite effect.

ELECTORAL SYSTEMS AND INTEGRATION

The extreme situations discussed above — when political systems come under stress — are not characteristic of the routine political behavior of normal electoral politics. Short of such dissident behavior — a mark of a disintegrating or at least weakened political system — the electoral process can play an important role as the citizen casts his ballot. His involvement with the political system is at least twofold. First, he votes for parties and candidates most favorable to those causes to which he is attached. He is integrated into the political system insofar as his particular interests receive the attention of the majority supporting the government, or at least insofar as the majority does not threaten his interests. The voter is able to identify with the government precisely because he feels that his act of voting has meaning in terms of specific protection which he receives from the government. Secondly, the act of voting itself integrates the voter into the political system. By playing a part in the political system which he conceives of as meaningful and useful, he is in a very real sense affirming his own role in the system. The act of voting brings him as close as he may ever come to the actual decision process, and that may be a very important political fact for the electorate at large.[4]

Both types of integration are present in almost all political systems, to some degree. No political system can exist for very long without some effort at placating specific dissatisfactions within the system, unless it wishes to impose arbitrary rule, and even then there will be efforts to satisfy local dissatisfactions short of forceful solutions. All systems, on the other hand, argue that supporters of the winning candidate as well as those who opposed are now equal before the government, that the sacred right of the franchise has resulted in a government of all the people, and that those who lost are merely momentary losers in the political war, that they will

---

[4] Feith notes in his study of the Indonesian elections of 1955, "To vote gave the villager a sense of importance, a sense of participation in something big. . . . And in what was probably a great majority of cases he could see that elections meant that he had the right to a choice between rival groups of his social superiors in the village which had clamored for his favor." Herbert Feith, "The Indonesian Elections of 1955," in Modern Indonesia Project, *Interim Reports Series* (Ithaca, N.Y.: Cornell University, 1957), pp. 52–53.

have their day in the next election and even before that time. What distinguishes election systems, therefore, is not the presence only of coalition building — what might be called the competitive element — or only of identification with the political system through voting — what might be called the element of participation — but both of these elements in different proportions. In single-party states with no competition some efforts to placate local dissatisfactions through an adjustment of candidacy or policy will be found; in competitive states total disregard for those who voted for the losing party is rare. Political systems may be categorized by a dominance of the participatory element, but neither element will be totally absent.

To examine the two integrating elements of elections more carefully, elections in two contrasting systems can be viewed: the Western party norm, specifically the plurality-system democracy, and the totalitarian state, specifically the Soviet system. To analyze only the results of election day in these two political systems — when the participation takes place and elite choice is expressed — removes the election from its rightful place in a much larger pattern of decision making. Elections do not begin — either in the West or in the Soviet Union — on the morning of election day, but begin formally months before, and forces at play may go back beyond the memory of any participant. Obviously, candidates must be nominated, and the choice of candidates is not made at the time of election, but days, perhaps even months, before. There must be a campaign of some sort so that the electorate is apprised of its responsibilities, perhaps given some of the arguments from which it will decide whom to support. In any election, without regard to the extent of "real" democratic involvement in the system, there must be a natural sequence of events: first the candidates who will contest the battle are selected; next the campaign in which the cues for the electorate are explored is waged; and finally the election itself in which the electorate either endorses the government in power or, in most electoral systems, has the opportunity to show its displeasure, takes place. The sequence may be confused by overlapping in the timing, the individual parts of the process may become more or less important between systems and between elections in the same system, the reality of the choice at any point may be suspect — but throughout all national elections some variant of this pattern is found.

The Western Norm: Party Democracy. In the politics of developed liberal democracies it is clear that the key element is party competition for election.[5] At each stage in the electoral process the electorate is involved, and each stage plays its own role in the resolution of political conflicts within a divided social system. Indeed, it is probably safe to say that a competitive-party system is the essence of Western democracy and that parties are the brokers that convert the election process into a coherent system, away from the referenda of "pure" democracy and toward the more intelligible competition of elites for power.[6] The party is probably primary actor in the process. Party nominates in the model system, party campaigns, and it is party that divides the electorate on election day, although independents may cause some confusion in this process.

The initial formal step is nomination. In general, it is certainly possible to argue that a party may nominate whomever it chooses, maintaining its own internal stability by presenting to the electorate its choice for nominee to be selected or not as the electorate so decides. In the competitive situation, however, any party habitually placing before the electorate candidates (no matter how acceptable to the party organization)

[5] Expressed most clearly in the concluding section of Sigmund Neumann, *Modern Political Parties* (Chicago: University of Chicago Press, 1956), esp. p. 395, as well as in his "Toward a Theory of Political Parties," *World Politics* 6 (July 1954), pp. 549–63. A more contemporary illustration of the importance of party to contemporary government is found in Roy C. Macridis, "Introduction," in Roy C. Macridis (ed.), *Political Parties* (New York: Harper & Row, 1967), esp. p. 9.

[6] For example, the late nineteenth-century Liberal party machine in the city of Birmingham, England, was once described in broker and connective terms: "It connects local ward interests with the general, social, and political life of the community." H. W. Crosskey, "The Liberal Association — the 600 — of Birmingham," *MacMillan's Magazine* 35 (1876–77), p. 304. See also Asa Briggs, *History of Birmingham*, vol. II (London: Oxford University Press, 1952), p. 172.

who are not acceptable to the electorate will be defeated. The party can in practice only nominate candidates for election which can hope to pursue a course to election. The essential assumption of party competition is that it will take care of those candidates who lack talent, interest, and style. The same is true of list proportional representation, in the sense that a number of unpopular candidates will be detrimental to the fortunes of the party as a whole and consequently will punish the party leadership by denying them the tools of legislative power. The implication of the assumption underlying a competitive party environment is that there is no strong argument against party control over nomination, since this political variation of the free market theory will effectively check the improper decisions of party nominating organizations.

The process of nominating standard-bearers is not that simple, particularly in plurality electoral systems. An obvious problem is the definition of a "good" candidate. Thus, the national leadership may define as desirable characteristics acquaintance with various national problems or prominence in national party circles. But for the constituency the definition may be quite different. While the long-range interests of the constituency may be better served by a candidate familiar with national matters, the short-term desires of the constituency may demand a candidate who is acquainted with local issues and local needs, who in his spare time may turn his attention from vineyards or coal mining or unionization to problems of war and peace or national reconstruction. While the party in its national wisdom may wish the selection of a prominent and nationally literate candidate, the constituency may desire a more locally oriented candidate who will attend the problems at home first. Therefore, in its efforts to seek the "good" candidate, the party must consider the merits of localism.

The party will be tempted to use the candidate as part of its campaign appeal, particularly in districts in which there is no sure majority for its cause. While many constituencies undoubtedly have single interests which will determine to some extent the candidate — it is only the very daring party which will offer to a lower-class, unionized constituency a member of industrial management as a candidate — many other constituencies have no single interest that dominates the constituency. Thus, by selecting a candidate from one interest in a constituency that is doubtful — say, a religious group that has political interests but no clear party loyalty — the party can appeal to that group in a manner that no amount of campaign oratory can match. A skillful assessment of a constituency may dictate exactly this tactic. Traditional supporters of the party in the constituency can be appeased on issue grounds or even with reminders of past benefits from the party, and wavering groups can be offered the concrete evidence of one of their own representing them in the councils of the party.[7] Such an appeal may not work, and indeed it may cause the loss of other slighted groups opposed to this nomination. But the opportunity for coalition building opens the way to success, though at the same time it places distinct limits on national party control of the party nominee.[8]

Offsetting this limitation on party nomination in marginal seats is the existence of numbers of relatively safe seats. Here is the national party's stronghold, where any candidate will defeat the most attractive and talented opposition. If the party

[7] One example of this type of appeal is noted in Frank Sorauf, *Party and Representation* (New York: The Atherton Press, 1963), p. 68: "The unsuccessful candidate tends to resemble the successful candidate . . . more than the victorious candidates of his own party running from other constituencies." While this observation is made about candidates for American state legislative seats, it is not certain whether similar patterns — though less marked — might be found in other two-party systems.

[8] This problem is explored in Henry Valen, "Factional Activities and Nomination in Political Parties," *Acta Sociologica* 3 (fasc. 4), pp. 183–99. It is interesting that Professor Valen pursues this study of one party of Norway that easily qualifies for the "divisive" role suggested by D. W. Rawson, "Domination in Party Systems — Mostly Australian," *Australian Journal of Politics and History* 10 (August 1964), pp. 173–82. Divisive parties are supposed to have less of a coalition-building orientation than integrative parties, although Professor Valen's observations would seem to suggest that even divisive parties must pay some attention to divergent factions. See also Robert E. Dowse and Trevor Smith, "Party Discipline in the House of Commons — A Comment," *Parliamentary Affairs* 16 (Spring 1963), esp. p. 164.

is limited in its choice of candidates in competitive seats, it is not limited here beyond some quite minimal political considerations. The party can use such safe districts for its faithful, as well as for its important, members in the sure knowledge that in any election save the most calamitous its candidates will emerge victorious. Under the best conditions the candidate may not even have to campaign beyond the most formal efforts, while the most stringent requirement may be the proposal of some new and attractive policy during the campaign in an effort to assure the local voters that a nationally oriented candidate has not forgotten them. In these districts the problems of coalition building within the constituency can safely be reserved for the campaign, if indeed there is any problem at all, and the district can be expected to return the appointed member on election day.

Although this discussion assumes the existence of a plurality electoral system, its conclusions can be applied to systems of proportional representation as well. In the list system, where the party receives as many seats from a formal list as its percentage of the popular vote deserves, the analogy to the safe seat is the top of the list, where only a complete disaster on election day will deny those fortunate members their seats. Since seats earned are usually counted off from the head of the list, the further down the name appears on the list, the more competitive the situation becomes until the last names on the list, virtually sure of losing or, to continue the analogy, absolutely unsafe, appear. Thus, it behooves the party constructing the list to include names that will prove to be local drawing cards as well as the names of those it wishes to be sure of election in order that local concentrations of strength will draw more votes to that party's poll.[9] Inclusion in the competitive part of the list is not only incentive to the candidate but is also important to his followers who may be attracted to his candidacy and thus to his particular party. In

[9] See, for example, Herbert Feith, *The Decline of Constitutional Democracy in Indonesia* (Ithaca, New York: Cornell University Press, 1962), p. 472, n. 13.

that sense a well-balanced list, between party sachems and locally desirable candidates, may prove to be a force for the molding of a successful coalition at election time.[10]

Between nomination and election stands the formal party confrontation, the campaign: the battle is in the open, the appeal to the voters is explicit, and the effort to construct the successful coalition begins in earnest as parties appear to explore the issues of the day and propose their solutions to a presumably interested electorate. These blandishments will always be at two levels — national and local — although, depending on the nature and competitiveness of the constituency, the emphasis will shift from one to the other. The proper balance of one element in the party appeal against the other will determine the success of the coalition attempt. Again, however, there are limits on what the parties may do in this part of the election process. First, the nature of the candidate himself may restrict the appeal that the party may make in the campaign. A candidate selected to appeal to one group in the constituency cannot then undertake to defend policies which may be detrimental to that group without alienating it. Further, a candidate selected with one appeal in mind — for example, one associated with restrictive immigration policies — cannot shift to an opposite pole and condemn policies with which he has been identified. On a cumulative basis the candidates will have considerable impact on national party behavior during the campaign, for the national image will have to be consistent with the image of individual candidates. Thus, the nominating process as a coalition-building device will limit the party during the campaign, itself a device of coalition building.

A second limitation on the freedom of parties in the campaign is the nature of the competitive situation in the close

[10] Uwe Kitzinger notes that one of the key problems in constructing the list aspect of German proportional representation since 1949 has been a balancing of "political orientation and efficiency" with interest decentralization; geography, sex, "Catholics and Protestants, workers and employers, the professional classes, farmers and traders all demanded consideration in a multi-dimensional balancing act." Kitzinger, *German Electoral Politics* (Oxford: Clarendon Press, 1960), pp. 68, 71.

constituencies. While the interplay of national and local issues will affect the behavior of the parties generally, the interplay of national and local issues will as well be important in the marginal districts that each party will endeavor to win. Each party certainly possesses safe districts which it can count upon, and each party faces certain defeat in other districts. But it is in the middle districts, where each party has the opportunity to win, that there exists the greatest pressure on parties to conform to local demands, or at least to local interpretations of national issues.[11] In order to capture these marginal seats a party must acquiesce to some degree to the centrifugal forces that are present in these districts lest another contender enter the contest and deprive the party of seats necessary to create the majority. The difficulty a party will have with this localizing tendency will be a function of several factors — how inconsistent the demands of marginal constituencies are with the demands of the traditional seats, how inconsistent marginal-seat demands are with national policy — but in each case the party must decide how far it will go in satisfying these demands or, to put it another way, how contradictory the interests forming its coalition will be allowed to become.

Despite the number of limitations on the behavior of parties in the electoral process, their primary effort is the construction and maintenance of coalitions of electoral support. The nominating and campaigning phases of the electoral process serve this end since their primary purpose is integrative in intent, although the number of alienated interests in even the most homogeneous societies would suggest that the effort is not always a successful one. Be that as it may, the nominating and campaigning phases of elections can be viewed as parts of the overall process leading to some form of majority agreement behind one party or coalition of parties

[11] It is perhaps true that ideological parties will resist the temptation to yield to the demands of marginal constituencies, but there may come a time in the life of the party where moderation becomes important. See, for example, the debate in *Encounter* over the future of the Labour party in England, particularly the issues of 1960–61; see also R. H. S. Crossman, "German Socialism Goes Democrat," *New Statesman* (December 3, 1960), pp. 864–65.

which will eventually be charged with the responsibility of governing. The ultimate test of this process of coalition construction is the election itself, in the formal act in which the population invests an elite with power that has been so carefully sought throughout the preceding phases of the electoral process.

Participation: The Russian Model. One very curious question for the amateur Kremlinologist exists: Why does a totalitarian system have elections, particularly elections in which the rules are so scrupulously obeyed and yet the outcome is foreordained.[12] Why does a powerful industrial nation, with a large and sophisticated population, go through the motions of casting ballots for a very large number of officials — perhaps in total as many as two million — with all of the trappings of elections, including ballot booths for unobserved marking of the ballots, locked election boxes, and careful checking of registration, when on the ballot there is only one party for each office, and rarely more than one candidate? The energy expended is considerable. The resources are not so plentiful that they may be thrown about in some casual pursuit of electoral games. Yet Russians go to the polls in numbers that shame the American voting turnout, and the Moscow leadership points with great pride to the tremendous support given the party at each election. It is confusing for the Western democrat, but it is not a unique pattern of schizophrenia; there are some useful lessons that can be drawn, and parts of the Soviet electoral process can be described in terms similar to those used in describing the Western model.

The most hostile interpretation that could be placed upon the election process in the Soviet Union is that it is totally for show purposes and for no other benefit.[13] Its propaganda value is perhaps of some utility to the regime, and certainly this fact is not lost on the leadership in its overseas campaigns.

[12] The question is well posed in Richard M. Scammon, "Why the Russians Bother with Elections," *New York Times Magazine* (April 6, 1958), pp. 14 ff.

[13] Such an analysis is found in K. Harasimewicz, "Elections — Bolshevik Style," reprinted in *Atlas* 2 (August 1961), pp. 128–29.

But this interpretation, as simple as it is, needs clarification. First, as the electorate becomes more knowledgeable about their interests — and even consumer oriented — the grave risk is run that these elections might come to have some importance for the voters, not as ratifications of the regime but as *elections*. Second, although it is difficult to perceive a government moving so far away from the sense of the people that it nominates candidates and pursues policies devastatingly unpopular with the masses, it is still possible, and elections might then become the focal point for a groundswell of opposition to the regime. Only use of terror by the governors could counter such a damaging blow as a massive rejection of the party. Third, as perhaps was the case in Poland in 1957, elections in even totalitarian countries can become the battleground for factional strife within the party, giving part of the leadership choice over to the mass population.[14] Thus, since elections in totalitarian states pose a considerable degree of risk to the regime, there must be clear and powerful advantages to be gained from the use of elections that transcend mere propaganda advantage.

In many respects the Russian electoral system under the post-Stalin period resembles the democratic model: the nomination of the candidate may be from among a number of contenders, although the party exercises control over the eventual choice; a campaign is conducted with local campaign "headquarters" with rather large staffs and considerable activity; and finally at election the voter has the opportunity to support or reject the candidates of the party. But whether each stage of the process — indeed whether the process itself — plays any significant, direct role in Soviet politics, is open to question.

First, it is useful to examine the process of nomination. Nominations for any soviet (the formal bodies of local government) are made formally at open meetings of representatives of constituency organizations, and the nominee must be sponsored by one of these organizations. A number of candi-

[14] Zbigniew Pelczynski, "Poland 1957," in D. E. Butler (ed.), *Elections Abroad* (London: Macmillan & Co., Ltd., 1959), pp. 119–79.

dates may be proposed for the nomination, although among
the names proposed may be that of the Chairman of the
Council of Ministers or some equally prominent luminary.
In any case, the meeting itself will not always be a ratification
of a single candidate from first to last; the appearance of
opposition may be at least maintained until the party leadership wishes to have the nominee declared.[15] At that time
"opposition" usually vanishes, and the nominee of the party
is selected from among the potentials. The mass nomination
meeting then accepts the nomination of the single candidate
unanimously, and the election campaign is well under way.
The unity of the system is preserved at the same time that
the individual, through his membership in one of the constituency organizations, is involved in the nominating process.

After the mass nomination meeting, there is no room for
public dispute about the candidate himself. But there does
seem some evidence that during the period before the actual
confirmation of the nominee there is at least the opportunity
for some efforts at rudimentary sampling of public attitudes.
First, in the several stages through which nominations go before the mass meeting, there is indeed the possibility of at
least clearing the prospective candidates with leadership in
each of the organizations in the district or the suborganiza-
tions within the whole local organization. Obviously, some
sentiment that might informally develop against a candidate
during this stage of the nomination process is wisely taken
into consideration, lest a momentary burst of unpopularity at
election time result in his defeat, a rare but not unknown phenomenon at the level of local soviets. Second, at the nomination meetings themselves there is the possibility of sampling
popular distaste, again through informal means, and there is
the formal means of actual public questioning of the candi-

---

[15] Howard Swearer, in "The Functions of Soviet Local Elections," *Midwest Journal of Political Science* 5 (May 1961), p. 141, suggests that several
candidates may be put forth from which one nominee is selected. However,
the rarity of this occurrence is suggested in Max E. Mote, *Soviet Local and
Republic Elections* (Stanford, Calif.: The Hoover Institution, Stanford
University, 1965), pp. 37–38.

date's fitness for office. For example, one observer has noted, "Particularly in recent years, the press has exhorted the people to make just criticisms and comments about candidates. Although there are powerful deterrents against criticism, including the carefully planned manipulation of meetings, if a candidate is intolerable, there may occasionally be an effective verbal revolt against him." [16] While it cannot by any stretch of the imagination be said that the nomination process is a popular one, in the sense of important mass participation, there are some techniques by which at least intensive non-party distaste for a nominee might be felt.

While elements of the nomination process might be seen as the beginnings of some form of coalition building, in general that is not the intent of the nomination process in the Soviet system and certainly not the practical function of the process. Rather, as a political device in an authoritarian state the nomination stresses a different aspect altogether: its central purpose is unification behind the party and ratification of the decisions of the state. But unity could be maintained through the simple presentation of a candidate at election time, without the bother of holding a mass meeting to accept a candidate already chosen by the party. Again, there must be some advantage other than merely the maintenance of unity combined with an occasional check on the popularity of candidates for leaders to take the risks that accompany mass participation. In our analysis the nomination technique used in Soviet elections is a device for involving citizens in government — not involving them in direct decision making but giving them a sense of identity through generalized participation.[17] The fact that numbers of people are involved through the use of a multistage device culminating in a mass meeting of, for example, a factory which will then endorse the single candidate, shifts the emphasis from that of nomination based

---

[16] Swearer, *op. cit.*, p. 143.

[17] The theme of popular participation is important in all Soviet life. See, for example, "Popular Participation in Government," reprinted from *Izvestia* in *Soviet Review* 1 (December 1960), pp. 68–70.

upon party fiat to that of nomination as a series of pro forma consultations with a large number of people who will give their consent to the nominee.

In that light the nature and results of the nominations become more intelligible. First, a reasonably large apparatus is involved in the selection of this happy contender, and the act of assenting to the nomination in fact creates in the individual some sense of identity with his candidacy and with the party and government. Second, the candidates themselves are not always "party men," though as Khrushchev noted to the 1958 American observer team, they will always be "reliable persons." Thus, the official title of the candidate group is the "Bloc of Communist and Non-Party People," indicating that the contenders are more than straight party functionaries. Third, nomination is not always for party service, and in fact is often a method of bestowing honor upon a popular hero or some individual who has gained stature outside of strictly party activity.[18] Finally, although each constituency in the end will have only one candidate, the practice of allowing at least for a short duration two candidates, one a genuine candidate, the other a national party leader, increases the involvement of the constituency with the national leadership and with the party itself. All of these factors broaden the party in form without yielding any substantial control over nomination procedures. In this sense the nomination technique can be viewed as a step in the process of political integration of the Soviet party, government, and people.

After nominees are registered, the actual campaign begins, and again the process emphasizes political integration much more than the presentation of arguments and issues. First, large numbers of people are involved in the process itself. Earlier, at the time of nomination, at least one agitator was selected for each candidate (candidates for the Supreme Soviet have even more than one) whose task, obviously, is to organize the subsequent agitation for the party and the candidate. Since there may be as many as 1.8 million local candidates for seats in local and Republic Soviets, already involved in the

18 Scammon, *op. cit.*, p. 63.

campaign are at least some four million people, and the campaign has barely begun.[19] During the campaign itself, run from *agitpunkts* (election headquarters in each polling division), numbers of volunteer agitators will radiate out through the constituency carrying the biography of the candidate and the message of the party to the electorate. From the agitpunkt, rallies are planned and the campaign itself is developed within the polling area; each voter is brought more into the campaign through contact with the organization. In fact, "an effort is made physically to weave every citizen to some degree into the campaign, which symbolically becomes the struggle of society to perfect itself and to overcome the enemies of communism." [20] Like the process of nomination, only now on a grander scale, the campaign involves people in, and identifies them with, the state.

Finally, election day comes. For those not already involved through the nomination process or the campaign agitation, there are multitudinous tasks to be performed. First, there are armies of election clerks for the day, so many that the American observer team reported that lines at the ballot box were rare and that by early afternoon in many precincts almost all voters had cast their ballots. Then there are the election commissioners of whom there may be as many as 8 million or more. There are also those workers in polling areas who are responsible for calling on those who have not already cast their vote or who need transportation to the polls. Finally, there is the large number of workers who aid voters with individual hardships — those who are hospitalized or who will not be in their home polling place and consequently need the "Certificate of the Right to Vote" in order to cast their ballot at any polling place near where they happen to be on election day. The number of individuals involved in the process is vast — an army [21] — but there remain those who have not partici-

---

[19] A tabular presentation of candidate numbers in the 1963 Soviet elections is found in Mote, *op. cit.*, p. 96.

[20] Swearer, *op. cit.*, p. 147.

[21] Mote, *op. cit.*, p. 101 suggests that for Leningrad alone there were 7,000 election commissions involving about 40,000 members.

pated in the system, who have not yet involved themselves with the party and the state. For these individuals there remains the act of voting, the act of formal assent to candidates who are chosen by the party and who will perform the will of the party. At the end of election day, millions will have been actively involved in the process, and between 99 and 100 percent of the voters will have cast their ballots. Indeed, the comment of one member of the American observer team is accurate, "Activity is a key word in Soviet life, and elections present maximum activity." [22]

Parallels, If Any, Between the Two Systems. Comparisons between democratic and totalitarian election processes are difficult to make, if for no other reason than that the elections take place within different social structures. There are single-party systems where there is considerable competition within the party for nomination; the American South or some of the single-party states of the underdeveloped world are examples. But even between these partially democratic systems and the totalitarian systems, the potential for opposition and the characteristics of the social structure are formidable barriers to comparability. In the norm of the democratic system the whole election process is geared toward the construction of voter coalitions, based on crude patterns of interest or reference group behavior. These groups of voters form subsystems of the electorate to which a party must appeal, and the election process is normally substantially influenced by the necessity to appeal to these groups of voters. While no totalitarian state may eliminate all ties between electors, their political relevance is diminished to the point that for all intents and

[22] Scammon, *op. cit.*, p. 64. See also Alfred G. Meyer, *The Soviet Political System* (New York: Random House, 1965), p. 274, where he suggests that "it is thus a day of dedication and rededication, the occasion for solemn confessions of faith and loyalty. The importance of such Holy Days for any political system should not be underestimated." See also Francis G. Wilson, "The Inactive Electorate and Social Revolution," *Southwestern Social Science Quarterly* 16 (March 1936), p. 80. An explicit comparison between one-party elections in developing states and the Soviet model is found in Aristide R. Zolberg, *One-Party Government in the Ivory Coast* (Princeton, N.J.: Princeton University Press, 1964), pp. 268–72, esp. p. 272, n. 73.

purposes the individual is without any identity paramount to his connection to the state. Thus, the social system itself determines that the primary appeal will not be to blocks of voters — which politically do not exist — but to the individual.

With this important variable in mind, there are parallels between the two systems, democratic and totalitarian. Both systems seek to integrate the individual into the political system. In the totalitarian case, it is the primary purpose. In the democratic state it is not the primary purpose, and it is not chiefly the product of state activity. The act of voting certainly does involve the individual in the affairs of the democratic state; and there can be no doubt that one residue will be a sense of involvement in the process of government. But it is primarily because candidates and parties must recognize the existence of social groups, modifying party programs to suit dissident demands, that group members are integrated into the political system. Perhaps the best illustration is to see the reverse case, where groups were not recognized by any party. Whether it be the Progressive farmer in the American Midwest, the petite bourgeois of Poujadist France, or the Scottish Nationalists, their radicalism demands that the system pay some attention to them, and their programs suggest a loss of confidence in the government and the inability of the existing party system to reach them and appeal to their interests. They have not been integrated into the political fabric of the system by the parties, and protest through a third party seems the only successful route to integration of their demands into the general political process. Finally, the campaign itself plays a role in integrating the democratic voter into the political system by apprising him of problems of, and solutions for, the society of which he is a member.

In totalitarian and democratic elections the process seems formally parallel, but the purposes and functions differ. There is some, albeit minuscule, effort in the Soviet state to allow mass influence over the lower levels of the elected elite — some opposition may appear during the nominating process, a few of the very large number of candidates may be defeated at the polls — although the emphasis of the election process is on political integration. In the democratic state there is some emphasis on integration though the main emphasis is on elite selection by the mass population. Between these two systems, balancing as they do elite acceptance and political integration, lie most of the political systems of the world.

COMPETITION, PARTICIPATION, AND INTEGRATION

In this chapter, the three stages of the electoral process — nomination, campaign, and election — have been examined in both competitive and participatory models of elections. The competitive model is derived from the British form, and it is applicable to those systems which indirectly derive their pedigree from Westminster as well as those which claim direct descent. Thus, though the electoral system of the Fifth Republic in form differs markedly from that of the British, it does not deviate from the model sufficiently to be anything but an amendment. In the Soviet system, one emphasizing mass participation, the three stages of an election play different roles. While in the competitive model, for example, campaign and nomination help the electorate to choose its elite, in the Soviet model, since only minimal attention is paid to elite control, campaign and nomination help create both an identity between party, state, and citizen, and tighter bonds within the society as a whole. Unlike the competitive model, the model of participation does not culminate in the election itself, for the election is only another technique for involving the mass population as a whole; it serves no separate function. There are of course intermediate forms, such as the single-party systems of developing states, which limit the electoral choice more severely than the competitive norm would allow, but allow enough choice so that some coalition building is possible. For example, the single party might control nomination proceedings by exercising a veto over candidacy but at the same time in the election allow competition between two candidates who are both party members and are equally acceptable to the party. In such a system, not unlike the form of the southern American primary, the voter is partially integrated into the decision process through the act of voting while a modest amount of attention is paid to political integration through the process of coalition building in the constituency. Elite stability is somewhat lessened, but integration of populace with party and state is furthered through both involvement and interest articulation.

The variables of national integration and elite control on the one hand, and representation of interest and governmental stability on the other hand, are inextricable. National integration may be accomplished through interest articulation and representation in the electoral process, but the cost may be legislative stability and cohesion in governing councils. To maintain stability and control, the Soviet system and other totalitarian states must resort to one-party politics. National integration must be pursued through different techniques, some electoral and some not — the national symbols, the parading of heroes, canonization of independence leaders, and the creation of external hostile forces. If, however, through democratic commitment or national decentralization, local articulation is a fact of life, necessary representation of interest may be accomplished at the cost of instability among the elite and consequent governmental instability. Various techniques are examined in this volume which deal directly with this complex problem.

Elite stability combined with a sense of integration characteristic of the Soviet model finds some counterpart in democratic states in the techniques of centralized candidate control of states employing party discipline within legislative bodies and in techniques for reducing the number of competing parties in states employing proportional representation. Whatever the structure of the electoral device, a state must constantly be aware of the dangers inherent in the representation of interest or in the disregard of interest. While to some extent all electoral systems limit the number of contenders, no electoral system can afford to limit beyond the point of rationality, lest the ignored call attention to their plight through appeal to the streets. All electoral systems must carefully walk a fine line — that between stability and representation — and the failure of any electoral system may be found in the commitment to overrepresentation or excess stability.

CHAPTER VI

Integration and Representation in Developing States

THE IMPERFECT NATURE of politics in developing states is perhaps their most salient characteristic. Politics is often the competition among elites for power within the confines of the capital city, while the hinterlands rest merely on traditional patterns of rule and authority with only an occasional breath from the new rulers in a capital light years away. Traditional patterns of decision making and traditional modes of life shape a society which is decentralized in structure but centralized in the patterns of decision making presented to the outside world. The seemingly dangerous conflict between partially integrated subsystems and a limited range of policy formation perhaps is the most important fact in considering the organization of political control, and more specifically in considering the organization of democratic control through elections. It is certainly too much to ask that the voter in any country be as well informed on issues and the shadings of policy as the man for whom he is to vote, but surely there is some doubt cast upon the validity of elections if there is no real understanding of the nature of the office being selected nor of the implications of casting a ballot for national president. The notion of an electorate attuned less to national concerns than to village and tribal problems is one that disturbs the more Western-oriented man.

The disparity between developed and developing systems is not so easily described. A number of electoral systems in the developed world must operate in environments that do not allow the centralization of legislative responsibility, a number of developed party systems operate in environments of discord not imaginable in most developing states, and a number of "modern" political systems have dynamic histories of groups violently in conflict. In fact, one might argue that the absence of consensus creates greater instability in a developed state than a developing one, and for two reasons. First, as the result of a long history of popular contact within an identifiable nation-state, demographic boundaries may be more easily identified, and the boundaries of conflicts have the legitimacy and bitterness of a history of tension without frequent parallel in developing states. For sure, there are conflicts between communal groups in developing countries, but these conflicts seem relatively fewer in number than those of class or ethnic group, and certainly are far less petty than conflicts frequently occurring in developed states. Secondly, out of the sense of nationhood in the developed state there emerges a sense of what national power is all about, and there may emerge a fear of how that national power can be used. The debate in France over forms of the presidency may suggest the stakes involved in the creation of national institutions and how these national institutions can be manipulated for the benefit of special groups. While it is clear that developing states often have parallel conflicts, again, they are not as numerous and they are less popular in their base. At the very most the conflict is between those who wish only to be left alone and those who wish to modernize; it is generally not over creation of national institutions for single interest purposes.

Beyond these rather general observations there are other parallels which are useful to pursue between the modern, yet nonconsensual, state and the developing state. First, as has been noted, the legitimacy of national institutions may be in doubt, though the difference is between distrust and ignorance. Secondly, the legitimacy of opposition may be equally suspect, though from polar points of view. In the nonconsensual state opposition is obviously the hallmark of popular politics, but not a united and joined opposition as is the case in their more consensual brethren. Opposition in the divided society is to institutions and forms of governing, and the idea of policy opposition within the accepted political framework may be suspect precisely because it is within the extant political system. In the developing state, on the other hand, opposition may be suspect because it is often confused with opposition to the nature of the state itself. Independence may be the keynote of the nation, yet different routes to post-independence goals may be thought to be rejection of the myth of independence, as exiled politicians from Senegal to Kenya may easily testify. Thirdly, the absence of any single, broad-based alternative to the governing party in power does little to develop the spirit of integration through opposition. As will be seen in the case of Turkey, for example, developing states may easily be able to convert to a multiparty system through careful adjustment of coercive tactics, while the developed state lacking consensus may find this step extraordinarily difficult and may find a long period of tutelary rule necessary before the development of a national consensus around national institutions.

The failure of national institutions to establish their legitimacy is perhaps the single parallel characteristic of developing and developed, but nonconsensual, regimes. Establishing legitimacy requires two concurrent developments: first, an effective regime which can deliver responses to important problems; and second, popular involvement through channels broad enough to encourage participation but narrow enough to encourage cooperation at the prepolicy stage. The first requires governmental stability; the second, representation and participation. Obtaining these in a developed state, where nonconsensual politics may have a long and bloody history, is perhaps more difficult than in developing states where leadership may have a residue of popular support generated from the successful independence movement, while leaders may have the additional advantage of making decisions that affect only tangentially the vast bulk of the population.

In each case, developed or developing, the absence of any nationally accepted institutions with their own inherent legitimacy — long-term attachment to parties of aggregation or to party alternation, for example — creates another problem: the possibility of sudden swings of popular will which can change policy and disrupt the nation. Accepted institutions are buffers against sudden change, and their absence may create conditions by which demagogic elites can seize power and influence to the detriment of the state. The alternative becomes those institutions of force — the army, the police — whose effectiveness rests less on their social legitimacy than on their own internal order and monopoly of force. The long-range outlook for the developing state, having to deal only with traditional resistance rather than entrenched suspicion of government based on historical experience, may be brighter than for those states which though developed have not perfected their own institutions. Perhaps the problem of mobilization is less thorny in traditional states than in those states where development has meant institutionalization, not of the tools of governing, but of the lines of separation.

MOBILIZATION

While the problems of mobilization are formidable in both developed and developing states, it is not at all clear that the nature of the problems are the same in each case. Styles of political and social interaction have emerged within developed states that may not be suitable as models for the understanding of problems of political development elsewhere. Thus, styles of participation — where allegiance to the state is the result of state-oriented activity — and of competition — where allegiance is generated through interest aggregation in a competitive party system — to some extent solve the problems of the industrialized world. They either discourage any activity other than state activity, as is the case in the Soviet participatory model, or they encourage the growth of societal subgroups by allowing for articulation and aggregation of interests through the party and electoral systems. The competitive party will serve to aggregate interests during elections in order that it might be the most successful of its breed, while the participatory party uses elections to wed the population more closely to the state and hopefully divert the population from potentially deviant escapades. In each instance party is related to interests that perceive a national government and a connection between that government and their own well-being.

Not all nation-states possess such a complexion of nationally oriented interests, and certainly not all states possess a complex pluralism capable of supporting a competitive, bargain-oriented party system. In fact, a pluralist social system may be the consequence of modern, developed societies that can afford the luxury of competitive party politics because they have the necessary rational identity and a general, if vague, consensus on the relevant range of questions. If these two elements are absent, the party system may have to follow lines of coercion to restrict the number and nature of questions put to the electorate while at the same time the electorate is taught the validity of the questions and the partial validity of the answers presented by the current elite. The party cannot forage out after a coalition of interests that will make its electoral victory, for there may not be a coalition of interests sufficiently large to yield a majority supportive of its national outlook. Nor, however, can it simply abdicate its democratic pretensions and impose its will through terror and coercion, if it wishes to leave behind it a substantially better prepared democracy. It is this effort, the communication of national value and national forms through a limited competition, that we can call a model of party as mobilizing agent. One of the most interesting recent examples is Turkey of Kemal Ataturk.[1]

Perhaps the best way to describe the dilemma of Ataturk and his military colleagues at the beginning of the 1920s is in a simple paradox: modernization or democracy. On the one hand, the elite was interested in developing a modernized Turkey, full of the forms of Western influence, notably,

[1] Turkey is perhaps the model of the successful mobilization system. See particularly David Apter, *The Politics of Modernization* (Chicago: University of Chicago Press, 1965), p. 405n.

religious emancipation, education, technocracy, and nationalism. In a nation where religion was established through a
sultanate, where women were in a vastly subordinate position,
and where traditional forms dominated a largely rural society,
such modern positions could only be adopted through a restrictive political system in which opposition would have
only a limited opportunity to unseat government and in
which the form of the state might not come into question.
The ease with which such a state might become authoritarian,
or even totalitarian, is apparent. On the other hand, there
seems to have been a genuine commitment on the part of
Ataturk to lead his nation to a higher state of preparedness
for the difficulties of democratic government, where party
competition might serve to broaden the basis for political
change.[2] In the reconciliation of these seemingly contradictory
goals three problems are worth investigation: first, the form of
popular participation; second, the role of the party as tutor;
and third, how the principle of opposition is maintained. In-
vestigating these three problems will perhaps shed some light
upon the role of party as national mobilizer in Turkey between the wars.

The form of popular participation in a state so divided as
Turkey in the 1920s and 1930s is of major importance for the
stability of the regime and the continuity of development. A
populist election system, such as proportional representation,
might result in a multiplicity of factions and a squabbling and
ineffective legislature. Multipartyism would be the order of
the day, and it would be the legislature which would be called
upon to reconcile the divisions at the same time that it must
provide the necessary formal support for government and
presidential election. But a single-member district system
would hardly be the answer, since most of the candidates
would either be the product of parochial interests or be imposed from the top by the party apparatus. Even in the latter
case there would be small guarantee of stability, for a candi-

[2] One of the major themes stressed in Donald Everett Webster, *The
Turkey of Ataturk* (Philadelphia: The American Academy of Political and
Social Sciences, 1939).

date who once believes that his constituency will support his opposition to party policy can be a severe nuisance to a dedicated elite, no matter how he was selected. Fortunately for the regime, a simple electoral device was available that solved a number of problems at once and had the additional advantage of having been used before.[3] A system of indirect elections in which the electorate votes for electors who then elect the members of the Grand National Assembly prevented the national divisions of proportional representation, isolated candidate from constituency, and facilitated party control. After popular elections, in which possible dissident elements had been filtered out by the form of the electoral system, a legislature could meet and contribute to the development of a tradition of legislative government.

The system of indirect elections has much to say for it as a device to further a tradition of stable institutions. But it is less than admirable as a device for inculcating responsible traditions of representation, in particular the delicate relation of representative to people. This is a fragile linkage, and one that needs more than good will to develop. Thus, from the perspective of the representative, the important instrument in his election is not his personal attraction as a candidate, but his party and its skillful organization and selection of electors to place him in power. His role in the legislature will be one of party concerns, for it is to the party alone that he owes his allegiance and not to any faction or local interest. The voter is also affected by this apparent party hegemony. His vote is cast for something other than a candidate or even for the party of a candidate, since he is merely voting for the first step in a two-stage device. He sees the party, but strictly within the confines of the election he does not see legislative party at all but the party of electors who link him only tangentially with all of the powers of government. He does not see his representative and at this stage may not even be aware who he will be, an advantage that his counterpart in list proportional systems certainly has. The voter must go on

[3] See Frederick W. Frey, *The Turkish Political Elite* (Cambridge, Mass.: The M.I.T. Press, 1965), appendix A.

the pure faith that party will serve him well, or the politician must go on the pure faith that the voter needs only party to maintain his allegiance to the nation.

It should immediately be noted here that the first principle developed is the party tie between citizen and legislature, and under the Turkish system that meant formally to all of government. This established linkage is no mean accomplishment in a developing society, and it can be very useful for the institution of social change. Obviously, since party was so important in the process of election, party also made great efforts to propagandize during elections, using elections as the basic teaching device familiar in more authoritarian regimes as well as more democratic ones. Leadership tours, such as those by Ataturk himself, were additional linkages to the citizenry, along with candidate selection that appealed to various highly identified groups in the society, notably, army and officials. But elections also served a more profound purpose, for it was through elections that some of the symbols of modernization were most graphically illustrated. Certainly, popular elections bring a sense of a new political modernity to the peasant areas, the existence of party apparatus in remote areas brings the presence of government, and the act of participation in elections brings home social changes in a powerful symbolism. For example, the emancipation of women in a Muslim culture may be no more heavily underscored than by the opening of the Turkish franchise to them, as was the case in 1935. The electoral process, while severely restricting popular participation as it is known in developed democracies, facilitated the development of a single national institutional linkage — the party — while it opened to the party the opportunity to propagandize and to use the electoral process to impress the process of modernization and change on the citizenry.

The interrelation of a stable government, popular participation, and democratic tutelage rests upon a difficult balance, that between coercion and allegiance. No society exists without an element of each of these two; but in a developing society, with vast numbers of centrifugal forces and few if any centripetal ones, the delicacy of the balance is less precise and the moral, psychological, and institutional obstacles to a violent swing in one direction or the other are less viable. Modernization and nation building require the establishment of allegiance amidst the constant threat of disintegration, and it is far too much to ask of election campaigns that they be the sole tool of national development. For this there are two sound reasons. First, election campaigns come infrequently, and they have a character of intermittent frenzy rather than a careful and sound construction toward the climactic expression of voting. Because they risk, in short, periods of over-stimulation followed by periods of long inactivity, in and of themselves they cannot create a national allegiance. As expressers of a national sense and feeling, they are excellent, precisely because of their infrequent nature, but they are not the building tools of a national identity. Secondly, and perhaps more importantly, without a process of education between elections, the campaign is meaningless. Elections are real events in developed nations precisely because they activate an existing sense of national identity; in short, it is a primary way of expressing nationality and the general level of approval of what the nation has done. At the same time, elections are also expressions of group attachments through voting for national leaders. All in the same action, a blue-collar voter may be indicating his acceptance of the American governmental system, his loyalty to the Democratic party, and his interest in supporting candidates who will further blue-collar interests. In the absence of these national links — direct, or indirect through group attachment — the election is meaningless unless it is tied to those widely shared values which are generally familiar to the voting public; and in a nonmobilized, developing society such values are usually those of traditional forms and beliefs. An appeal to such values may be dysfunctional to the emergence of nation-voter links, and they will certainly be counterproductive to the emergence of a sense of popular participation in, and approval of, the process of modernization.

Beginning in 1932, perhaps with the realization that good

works and election propaganda were not sufficient stuff for
nation building, the People's Republican party of Turkey
established a series of local organizations for the purpose of
bridging "the gap between the intelligentsia and the people
by teaching the first of these the national culture which lay
among the Anatolian masses and the second, the rudiments of
civilization, and an indoctrination of the nationalist secular
ideas of the Republican regime." [4] From the beginning the
culture associations, or "People's Houses," had about them the
strong air of political indoctrination; and, had the initial goal
of establishing 500 associations been reached, they would have
proved a formidable method for communicating the general
and immediate goals of the regime. While these associations
were less than absolutely effective, both in number established
and in content, they were an effort to communicate across a
broad range of cultural, economic, and political concerns
which would begin to fill the gap between the cultural identity necessary for the modern integrated state and the particularism of the Turkish population. Ataturk provided the
national symbol of modernity (he wore a hat rather than a
fez, for example, and was something of a night club buff),
party provided the political linkage and the occasionally
necessary political coercion, elections provided the time for
expressions of participation and occasions for popular education, and such efforts as the People's Houses and the smaller
People's Rooms provided the political-cultural glue that eventually might provide the underpinning for the whole endeavor. The educational functions of elite, party, elections,
and cultural organizations led a step further away from coercion toward allegiance as the basic component of the state,
while at the same time substructures which might be more
effective brakes upon the behavior of the state were developed.

The third problem — how to maintain the principle of opposition — reveals the true difficulty of instilling democracy
through centralized control and education. Even if the elite
and party successfully develop participation, and if political

---

[4] Kemal H. Karpat, "The People's Houses in Turkey," *Middle East
Journal* 17 (Winter-Spring 1963), p. 55.

education brings about a greater degree of popular identity with state and with modernization, the political system will be gravely truncated in the absence of a tradition of opposition. In the case of Kemalist Turkey at least three different forms of opposition existed during the interwar period, although with varying degrees of success. The first form, tried first in 1924 and more systematically in 1930, was an organized party of opposition. Immediately, and most clearly with the Liberal party in 1930, the opposition party became the focal point for the range of grievances within Turkey against the state, from policy divergences to very conservative reaction against secularization and modernization; and within a few months the effort collapsed. Control was reinstituted, and the single party entered a stage of reaction against the possibility of external opposition until the process of political education was better developed.[5] (It is no coincidence that within a year the plans for the People's Houses were underway.) As an aftermath of the Liberal party incident of 1930 and in some sense as a response to external and internal pressure for at least the form of parliamentary democracy, a second effort at institutionalizing opposition was attempted in the form of a loose group of independent members — thirty, elected by write-in ballot — who were later brought together into a formal organization of independents in the legislature. Their number and their character made them ineffective as opponents, since quite obviously they would never be able to form a cabinet under the Kemalist regime that would be substantially different from the prevailing line of the People's Republican party, but their presence was an unmistakable "device for accustoming people to the operations of a multi-party regime." [6]

While the existence of opposition, no matter how forlorn, suggests to the populace that such an institution is desirable and that it is customary, its salutary effect does not cease with the populace itself. The presence of an officially sanctioned

[5] Kemal H. Karpat, *Turkey's Politics* (Princeton, N.J.: Princeton University Press, 1959), pp. 64–68.
[6] Frey, *Turkish Elite*, p. 345.

opposition has an influence on the party as well, and that influence may in the long run be as important as the influence on the people at large.[7] Parties are composed of activists, who presumably will be in power regardless of the form of the state; and if the activists come to tolerate the opposition, that institution is much safer. Both forms of opposition mentioned thus far play an educative role for both populace and party, though probably in different proportions and in different emphases. The presence of a disciplined opposition party, perhaps disrespected by the majority party activists, goes a long way toward implanting in the popular mind the acceptability of opposition. The second form, the presence of a cluster of independents, is far less visible to the electorate but far more visible to the party in power. Given their character — they tended to be luminaries and intellectuals — their presence would be felt more in debate than would the activities of a second party, and their criticisms would sting the more, their source being in disinterest rather than in the hopes of succession. The third form of opposition — dissident factionalism within a party — is surely more for the party than for the people, although internal factional battles cannot be concealed entirely. The willingness to tolerate dissident factionalism within a whole party structure is a painful lesson but one that may be the most important single step a ruling elite can take on the road to democracy. It is possible to establish the internal pluralism of the party in two separate manners. First, there may be a feud between two political rivals, as there was between Celal Beyar and the future president and successor to Ataturk, Ismet Inonu. They disagreed about an active versus a passive role for government in the economy.[8] The conflict even had a regional bias, as Inonu tended to ignore the Aegean area during his presidency, while Beyar tended to lean toward the Aegean area.[9] Secondly, pluralism may be

[7] Cf. Walter F. Weiker, *The Turkish Revolution, 1960–1961* (Washington, D.C.: The Brookings Institution, 1963), p. 5.

[8] Karpat, *Turkey's Politics*, pp. 69–70.

[9] Frey, *Turkish Elite*, p. 275.

evidenced by a lack of punishment for party dissenters; in the feud just cited opponents of the party's rule were treated rather harshly, but dissent inside the party was not punished and there seemed to be no real ground rules for purging. In a very real sense, "as factions develop freely inside a single party this becomes simply a framework which limits political rivalries without destroying them; prohibited outside the single party, pluralism is reborn inside the party, and there it can play the same part." [10] Whether one points to the presence of long-term factional wars within the party or to the absence of general rules and procedures for expulsion from the party councils (for anything but counterrevolutionary behavior), there is little question that the party learns to live with a degree of diversity that may prove advantageous in future years when the single party is replaced with a formally more diverse political system.

The success of popular participation, of the party in its role as tutor, and of maintaining the principle of opposition may be measured by the kind of popular control the electorate is able to exercise over the government. It was a matter of some pride that the regime held elections and that elections renewed the party's mandate every so often. That pride was not incidental. If the party of mobilization is to succeed in its most difficult tasks, which means simultaneously succeeding in rulership, education, and eliciting political response, it must leave behind it a tradition which can be readily translated into popular control through elections. During the period of elections themselves, the party must perform as though it were in a competitive pattern for no other reason than the necessity of leaving behind it such a tradition. The elections provide the unique opportunity for the single-party state to mobilize its citizens to express their approval, to participate in the affairs of state. At no other time in the life of the democratic state that hopefully will follow will the electorate be so motivated to react as one; but that reaction will be

[10] Maurice Duverger, *Political Parties* (New York: Science Editions, 1963), p. 278.

interpreted and understood in terms of the tradition that the mobilization party has laid down, both as an integral part of the electoral process and as the party of government.

REPRESENTATION

In the effort to forge a unity of political interest and activity nations must create national institutions with a legitimacy that transcends parochial and ascriptive-traditional attachments. One technique is through the party system and the consequent elections that tie the political system into a whole by uniting interest with institution and relating the policy preferences of the elite to popular mandate. In this process of creating a whole — what has by implication been called mobilization — specific group identities must yield before the onslaught of unification and integration, because they appear to be dysfunctional to the ultimate goal of the state. Two problems emerge in this process. First, there is the simple problem of coping with traditional patterns of behavior that may be well entrenched and whose upset may cause repercussions too vast for the as yet unstable new state to control. The care with which old theocratic principles are overturned or the delicacy with which traditional forms are often maintained — certain African rituals of coronation, for example — testifies to the durability of these traditional modes and their capacity to resist the most reasonable of new proposals. The second problem is of a different order, namely, determining which demands for protection are necessary and which are not. Certain traditional barriers must fall — perhaps language and those against travel — along with codes conferring subject status to certain citizens but not others. Other codes, however, may have to be protected against the incursions of the central authority as too sensitive for the casual manipulation by government, and their protection creates peculiar problems for new states. These are usually codes of social customs, such as religion, race, or tribe. The protection of religious or ethnic subsystems from the hostility of the remainder of the society — necessary to gain the inclusion of the group in the first place — creates problems that may only be handled through protective measures found in federal or electoral techniques.[11]

PROBLEMS OF REPRESENTATION

If the only difficulties faced in developing states were vast illiteracy combined with physical debilitation as a result of environment, then perhaps the study of developing nations would be less interesting than it really is. In fact, part and parcel with Responsible Government and the imported traditions of Europe came the imposition of national lines and political subdivisions in style to fit the inclinations of the colonialists, and usually these boundaries were not coterminous with ethnic, linguistic, or economic boundaries. Further compounding the difficulty, most areas of the world have as one demographic feature colonies of nomadic tribesmen who wander neither knowing nor caring about the political divisions that mark maps but not landscape. Granted, some lines were traditional and realistic — the Zambesi or the Himalayas, the Andes or the Great Lakes. But more often than not the lines were drawn from point A to point B with less reference to whether the inhabitants south of AB had more in common with those north of that line than they did with their fellow southerners. If to all the other problems of these struggling societies is added the complex of antagonisms that surrounds racial, ethnic, or religious hatred, then indeed the system will have grave difficulties.

Within this general distribution of cultural groups, we find two major cultural types. First, the plural elements of the society may be merely competing indigenous groups, some or all of which may have been immigrants from surrounding areas, but which have in common a lack of experience with developed political forms — no acquaintance with, nor

[11] An added complexity in the new states is the importation of electoral systems rather than their home cultivation. "The only thing that can be predicted with certainty about the export of elections is that an electoral system will not work in the same way in its new setting as in its old." W. J. M. MacKenzie, "The Export of Electoral Systems," *Political Studies* 5 (October 1957), p. 255.

heritage of, some variety of traditional political organization. Thus, nations such as Ceylon, India, South Africa, and most of the multitribal African states all have in common a pluralism based upon indigenous cultural groups that share an affinity with the traditional and a distrust of, or at least unfamiliarity with, the modern world. Also found in most of these plural societies is the second major cultural type, the settler or the colon, who is from the modern world, is familiar with its political ways, and who probably wishes to adopt most of its techniques for national government. His patterns are definitely extensions of the modern world — his papers may come from London, his children are educated in Europe, his vacations are spent in his "homeland," and so on — and he maintains his norms to the degree that the colonial environment allows him. The crunch comes when decisions about voting qualifications and the rights of citizenship have to be made. The colon's definition of what is political man and the local definition are likely to come into severe conflict; and the colonial authorities, who are the settler's countrymen and in whose hands lie the primary responsibility for deciding such questions, are perhaps inclined to give their ethnic colleagues more than their fair share of representation.[12]

The political ramifications of social pluralism are compounded by the general distribution of contending cultural groups. First and most common is uneven geographical distribution of contentious groups within the nation, adding ethnic, religious, or linguistic communalism to the forces already tending to sectionalism. Thus, for example, by the middle of the nineteenth century the division into Upper and Lower Canada was also roughly a division between French

[12] Rhodes' criteria for equal rights are quite different from the criteria for simple citizenry: "My motto is, equal rights for every civilized man south of the Zambezi. What is a civilized man? A man whether white or black who has sufficient intelligence to write his name, has some property or work, in fact is not a loafer." Quoted in W. K. Hancock, *Survey of British Commonwealth Affairs*, vol. I (London: Oxford University Press, 1937), p. 188, n. 1.

and English Canada, an ethnic conflict only adding fuel to existing economic and historical difficulties.[13] In a similar case, that of Nigeria, the rough coincidence of ethnic lines and provincial boundaries made separatism possible and perhaps laid the foundation for the resultant civil war and disintegration of the state.[14] The geographical concentration of potentially hostile groups provides a ready demand for a decentralization of decision making, although simultaneously it provides additional intensity to the conflict between sections, each attempting to maximize its own share of the national resources. One answer to the potential instability resulting from such an intense and potentially hostile sectionalism is the federal principle, division of the nation into semisovereign states, each of which has reserved to it powers not allocated totally to the national government. Presumably, the distribution of powers will be balanced in such a manner that social groups will be able to control regional issues — religious, educational, and so on — at the state level, while matters of defense, national development, and the like will be concluded at the national level. Since regional issues are handled by governments of homogeneous states in the federation, the form of election need not be altered for the protection of minority rights. The question of electoral type becomes somewhat academic, because there will presumably be a relatively high degree of identity within the region and a single-member district system will be as satisfactory as anything else. A geographical distribution of dissident groups, therefore, will not necessarily need any special electoral arrangements provided the federal principle is adequately applied.

The other representational problem which pluralism may present is difficult to solve in any way but through the elec-

[13] According to Lord Durham's report, the population of Upper Canada was 400,000 English, of Lower Canada about 150,000 English and 450,000 French. Sir C. P. Lucas (ed.), *Lord Durham's Report on the Affairs of British North America* (Oxford: The Clarendon Press, 1912), p. 307.

[14] A parallel fear was expressed in the Canadian case. Lord Durham was concerned that federalism would lead to French nationalism at the local level. His recommendation was a "legislative union," a unitary parliamentary system which would prevent French rule in any parts of Canada. *Durham Report*, p. 296.

toral system. Although federalism may indeed be the answer for groups geographically concentrated, groups may also be distributed at random throughout societies. Or even if they are not so distributed but instead are concentrated at points throughout the system, each individual concentration may be too small to create a separate state for their protection. In this case, federalism is no solution. Unless they can find some beneficent larger group with which to form coalitions, dispersed minorities may simply become lost in the shuffle of politics, constantly on the short end of every controversy involving their interests.[15] Examples that immediately come to mind are tribal minorities in some of the smaller African states, Asian minorities in East Africa, or even the Muslim minority in India. All these groups have the same problem: identity within the confines of a larger, hostile society, without any political protection for their long-range interests in the form of some federal arrangement. While these concentrations of individuals are too small for federal status, they can be collected together nationally through electoral devices that either allot seats of the national assembly to these groups, or allot a certain number of seats to these groups which are listed on a separate voter roll and for all intents and purposes are part of a separate electoral process. Both of these techniques are used, as well as the implementation of federal devices, to protect minorities.

THE FEDERAL DEVICE

The unhappy experience of recent African states, notably Nigeria and the Congo, has beyond question challenged the utility of federalism as a device for minority protection. The principle of federalism is based upon two assumptions: first, that the differences between geographically isolated groups are significant and that any of them might be suppressed by

[15] The advice of T. O. Elias to the proposed West Indies Federation is pertinent: "But the communities are very often mixed communities, and experience elsewhere has shown that it is prudent to provide in advance for some of the imponderables of political independence after British power has been withdrawn from the Caribbean area." *Federation vs. Confederation and the Nigerian Federation* (Trinidad, 1960), p. 25.

coalitions of the others; and second, that there is enough national identity to make creation of a distinct nation worthwhile. Federalism is a balance between pressures pulling the nation apart and those pulling it together. In the nature of this balance are some implications for the representative nature of the political system itself.

In the first place, it is rare that any geographical section of a nation is the pure fief of one and only one cultural group. Quebec in the nineteenth century and at the present time is mostly — but not entirely — French Canadian, and the same is true of other federations of cultural groups. The Nigerian northern region under the old federation was predominantly Muslim and Hausa, but there were numbers of Ibo and Yoruba tribesmen, mostly non-Muslim, as well. Since the division of the nation into regions was supposedly to separate cultural groups into units that could govern themselves on sensitive issues, at the state level there may be few effective guarantees for these local minorities. In fact, since the federal device is supposed to be more effective than some form of electoral protection for minorities — such as proportional representation — the type of electoral system used in state elections will probably be a system which assumes social homogeneity within the state and whose major concern will not be representation but the preservation of a united state front against groups from other regions. Thus, plurality can be used effectively in these situations where minorities have their own cultural regions. But the existence of dissident subgroups within these large cultural regions suggests the possibility of a very large degree of underrepresentation for these minorities.[16] And the perhaps less than gentle treatment accorded these state minorities may feed fires in other regions that potentially can have disastrous effects upon the whole nation. The

[16] There is the note in the Nigeria minorities commission report that suggests these minorities had no fear of the Federal Government, "partly no doubt because the Regional Governments deal with matters which affect most people much more closely." *Report of the Commission Appointed to Enquire into the Fears of Minorities and the Means of Allaying Them,* Command 505 (1958), p. 2, hereafter cited as *Minorities Report* (Nigeria).

federal principle, employed as a device for the protection of minorities, may have something of the opposite effect, as indeed it did in Nigeria and the former Belgian Congo.[17]

The same general line of argument applies to national representation. Since the states of the country are assumed to be cultural entities of their own, there is little need for any electoral device at the national level to ensure the protection of minorities. Proportional electoral techniques, designed expressly for representation of minorities that are not able to achieve fair district representation, need not be employed. Thus, the local subgroup which cannot be an effective part of the state government may find recourse denied at the national level by a constitution whose basic assumption is the compartmentalization of the nation into homogeneous regional states. Again, the example of Nigeria is instructive. Although a definite region was created for the Ibo tribe, some members of this tribe were found as well in the northern region and became the object of increasing hostility from the Muslim Hausa majority. Their recourse at the regional level was minimal since regional politics were totally under the control of the dominant Hausa. On the other hand, the national government, where Ibo representation was guaranteed from the eastern region, was unable significantly to affect the fate of these minorities precisely because most minority affairs were under control of the regional governments.[18] The only alternatives in such a dilemma are migration to the home region of the tribe or existence in an unpleasant situation.

Federalism as a protective device for minorities leads to another difficulty perhaps more serious than the oppression of selected local minorities. As an integrative device, it leaves much to be desired. Since representation within the regions,

[17] The Durham Report argues, in fact, that a nonfederal form will force the French Canadian into the national fabric. *Durham Report*, p. 307.

[18] The rough distribution gave the central government control over external affairs, defense, and communications in the broadest sense, implying railways and the like; the "Regional legislatures have residual powers of legislation in respect of their Regions. . . ." *Minorities Report* (Nigeria), p. 4.

or states, is primarily not concerned with minoritie ;, and
since proportionality is achieved only between regions in national elections, at the national level only ephemeral coalitions, composed of regional parties, are formed, with little
pressure toward a broadly based party system that might concern itself with the destruction of cultural boundaries between groups.[19] Politics is a sectional game, and there is little
point in moving beyond that mode into a more national one.
Thus, as a device for the integration of groups into the political system, and even for the protection of local minorities,
federalism fails to create the necessary homogeneity or national identity that might serve as a structural glue to bind
the entire political system in times of stress. In that sense,
federalism serves only to perpetuate the status quo, until such
time that centrifugal forces become too intense for the nation
to remain together.[20]

If federalism is less than successful as a device for the protection of minorities, it is reasonable to look for protection
in the electoral system. While one speaks of federalism as a
protective device, it is merely another form of representation,
namely, that government should take into account the wishes
of sizable minorities in the political system whether or not
they have the power, influence, or inclination to be heard
through regular political channels. That all interests in a society should be heard is another way of saying that all interests in a society should have some form of protection, for
which federalism is one device. Thus, if the federal technique
is insufficient, perhaps the other institutionalization of minority benefit, some form of proportional representation,
should be attempted through the electoral system. In each
case the effort is the same: to take highly group-identified
individuals, interested at the moment in community goals

[19] In the long run it was probably most unfortunate that the commission did not "necessarily accept" the proposition "that the present majority
groups will always vote as solid blocks or that they will always seek to
use power to their own exclusive advantage." *Minorities Report* (Nigeria),
p. 2.

[20] Compare Eme O. Awa, *Federal Government in Nigeria* (Berkeley:
University of California Press, 1964), pp. 315–16.

more than national ones, and develop from that situation a system where basic political questions are decided with at least some reference to a broader national interest. The ideal electoral system would appear to be one which is decentralized enough so that community-oriented voters will not be alienated but will eventually be brought into the political system to think, act, and vote in noncommunal terms while at the same time their interests are protected against larger groups. It is no wonder that a large number of new states have turned to the electoral system to attain this extremely delicate balance.[21] Two alternatives have been tried: first, some form of guaranteed representation, and second, proportional representation.

Guaranteed representation parallels proportional representation, although it is obviously more rigid. With both systems the minority is represented regardless of how few votes are cast for it and regardless of how widely scattered these votes may be. Guaranteed representation differs from proportional representation in that the number of seats that a minority may win has little or nothing to do with the immediate rise or fall of votes, since the number of seats the minority is to receive will have been established well before the election and that number of seats may not be even closely related to the proportion of the population that the minority represents. Thus, for example, the protected status of the French national in West Africa was vastly inflated by the proportion of territorial assembly seats guaranteed through the double college system (one for French, one for African subjects), of course to the detriment of adequate African representation.

With guaranteed representation a segment of the population is isolated and awarded a fixed number of seats through a communal or geographic formula. Thus, for example, in parts of British Africa each of several communities — European, Asian, African — is awarded a number of seats and separate voting rolls are established for each of the racial candi-

[21] An exploration of many of the difficulties and promises of plural representation is W. J. M. MacKenzie, "Representation in Plural Societies," *Political Studies* 2 (February 1964), pp. 54–69.

dates. A voter on the African roll was allowed only to vote
for African candidates to fill the number of seats allotted to
the African majority, Asians for the Asian seats, and Europeans for European seats.[22] On the other hand, geographical
techniques would simply guarantee to an area — and consequently to the indigenous population — a certain number of
seats without immediate regard for the number of persons in-
habiting the area. The Ceylonese "honest gerrymander" allocated one seat for each 75,000 persons or for each 1,000
square miles, thus protecting the rurally based Tamils from
the more densely concentrated Sinhalese. Although numerous
forms exist of these two basic patterns, most involve the identification of a specially protected group or groups, the grant-
ing of special representation in the legislature, and the strict
control over that representation by the selected group or
groups. Guaranteed representation is designed to protect the
minority and to allow it to participate without fear in the
electoral process of its nation.

The advantage of guaranteed representation is obvious:
minorities are represented regardless of how they are distributed in a majority community, and absolute communal
power over that representation exists. The lines between
communities are clear and distinct, and in the act of voting
there can be no claim of improper electoral districting or
fraudulent counting. Implicit in this description, however, is
the first and major problem of guaranteed representation: [23]
the only integration that can take place within the political
system is at the very top, in part within the confines of the
legislature, as the representatives from each of the communi-

22 The general problems of separate rolls are briefly discussed in Sir
Ivor Jennings, *The Approach to Self-Government* (Cambridge, Eng.: Cambridge University Press, 1956), esp. pp. 92–93. Jennings notes that separate
rolls, by removing crosscommunal electoral competition illustrate acceptance of the "two nation" theory.

23 The Donoughmore Commissioners came to the conclusion that pure
communal representation had, in Ceylon, grave disadvantages. The result
of Ceylon's experience: "The evils of communal representation have ac-
centuated rather than diminished racial differences. . . ." Quoted in The
Hansard Society, *Problems of Parliamentary Government in Colonies* (London: The Hansard Society, 1953), p. 67.

ties come in contact with each other. Because there is no need for them to become politically aware of each other once seats have been allocated, communication may be difficult and there will be little popular understanding of different political needs among the various communities. There is obviously no manner in which one community can easily campaign against another, nor is there any convenient manner in which campaigning on a noncommunal matter may take place across the separate electoral communities. In short, there is no need for electoral cooperation among grass roots organizations leading to national integration or an understanding of politics above that of the community. The separate roll becomes a system by which the electorate is compartmentalized — in some systems more intensely than in others — in the interests of preserving minority rights, and in that interest the separation may become a permanent feature of the political landscape. A political device whose planned function is the political integration of the nation may develop into a dysfunctional element of considerable magnitude.

In institutional terms as well guaranteed representation through the electoral system may be less than commendable. If it is assumed that one of the primary disadvantages of the developing state is the absence of an established set of institutions with their own historical legitimacy, tampering with the electoral system may implant the idea and establish an unhealthy precedent. In the case of the honest gerrymander, for example, the proposition that electoral systems should be manipulated for the advantage of a single group, no matter how deserving, is not an easy precedent to dismiss. Even though there is no history of the institution to contend with, there is the difficulty of convincing a minority that they have been protected long enough. Indeed, if a favored minority is given majority power, as happened in British Africa, there may be considerable effective opposition to the termination of protected status, and opposition may cause severe internal stress in the colony or newly independent country.[24] Guaran-

---

24 Perhaps the clearest example was the system in Kenya in 1920 to 1944 and beyond, in which the white roll elected eleven members of the

teed representation, like federalism, may continue past its due date of retirement and may bring along a host of unwanted centrifugal forces that can postpone indefinitely the political integration of the independent nation.

PROPORTIONAL REPRESENTATION
IN PLURAL STATES

Fixed representation for communal groups in developing societies is analogous to proportional representation in developed states. In each case there is representation by groups rather than by legal constituency or some other criterion, although perhaps the more important parallel is the absence of any effort to reconcile conflicting interests except in the legislature itself. In plural developing states there is a strong argument for application of the principles of proportional representation. First, these states are not easily divided into single-member districts of distinct size and shape, since natural political boundaries often do not exist. Second, the impact of the single-member district system on losers not used to the sporting rules of Eton and Harrow might be quite severe, as they demand to know why they do not achieve representation although their party received a part — but not a plurality — of the vote. But the overriding concern is the characteristic that makes them plural states, namely, the multiplicity of races or communities composing their population. There must be some formula for representation of groups that will be ac-

---

legislative council, the Indian roll elected two to five members, Arabs none and later one, and Africans (the vast majority) elected none. G. F. Engholm, "African Elections in Kenya, March 1957," in W. J. M. MacKenzie and Kenneth Robinson, *Five Elections in Africa* (Oxford: The Clarendon Press, 1960), pp. 391–99, esp. table 4. The major franchise change before independence was the Coutts (or "fancy") franchise, allowing some voters three votes, others two, and most one vote, based on a series of qualifications designed to enhance the political power of the more modern African voter. See Marion Elizabeth Dore, "Kenya: A Case Study of the Development of Western Political Institutions in a Plural Society" (unpublished Ph.D. diss., University of Pennsylvania, 1959), pp. 199–216. For opposing statements on the limited franchise see the debate over reserving the Rhodesia-Nyasaland Electoral Bill of 1958 in *Federation of Rhodesia and Nyasaland: Electoral Bill, 1958*, Command 362 (1958).

cepted by most of the relevant communities of the nation. For this latter reason a number of authors have proposed the use of some form of proportional representation in these developing states with pluralist societies.[25]

Even so, the number of states experimenting with proportional techniques has on the whole been rather small. There are certainly valid historical reasons for this, particularly since most of the countries to achieve independence in the period after the Second World War were of either French or British colonial heritage, and neither of these two nations has shown a marked and sustained commitment to proportionality. Further, the simplicity of the single-member district system is perhaps of greatest value in a state where communalism may exist coincident with illiteracy and political inexperience. Perhaps of equal importance the single constituency lends itself to regional and local organization in a manner far superior to a list system of proportional representation, requiring as it does that either national or large regional parties put together lists of candidates. It is possible that the single local constituency be easily organized and contested, particularly in rural areas, but in the cities it is more difficult to separate out communities one from another. Finally, even in states which have been able to develop national parties of some degree of cohesion and consistency, it is undoubtedly easier to work from a local base in the village to one local constituency than it is from village to district and then to region, in order to organize the party to contest elections.

This is not to say that proportional techniques have not been employed in Asia and Africa but only that the plurality system has been the more usual method of electing legislatures. Both varieties of proportionality have been employed, although the single transferable vote has been used primarily in special circumstances, usually the election of one legislative body by another, as in the case of the Senate of Ceylon which

---

[25] For example, J. A. LaPonce, "The Protection of Minorities by the Electoral System," *Western Political Quarterly* 10 (June 1957), pp. 318–39. W. J. M. MacKenzie, *Free Elections* (London: George Allen & Unwin, Ltd., 1958) generally endorses the single transferable vote.

is elected by the lower house. The transferable device has been employed on the island nation of Malta since 1921 in popular elections, although with somewhat inconsistent success even though the population is a literate one. The Maltese experience has indicated that the transferable vote opens the way to the development of strong followings by local leaders which can be converted into support for candidates in elections. The inevitable results are two: first, bed sheet ballots occur because each local leader with any strength is able to contest the elections as an independent; and second, politics become personal rather than party oriented, to the detriment of any sort of efficient national political organization. The experience of Malta suggests that the single transferable vote is ineffective as a coalition-building device and results in a disintegration of the entire political party framework.[26]

The list system of proportional representation is perhaps more easily used, particularly if there are strong dividing lines between communities. First, it is a very simple election system for illiterate voters. Each party need only be assigned a symbol or color, and the voter merely selects the symbol or color of the party of his choice. Secondly, as J. A. LaPonce has pointed out, it is perhaps the only successful system if parties are organized on a communal basis,[27] especially if the dividing lines are such that little communication between the contending communities is possible. In this case proportional representation would reflect the distribution of interests in the society; the only possible compromises would be made by the representatives in the legislative assembly. While the advantage to be gained from proportional representation is the possibility of a state existing at all, it should be noted that there would be little pressure for the parties to move away from communalism. Finally, since list systems use either the nation or at least very large regions for constituencies, the influence of village or clan attachments is reduced and the divergent tendencies of the electorate is raised at least to the level of

[26] Jeremy Boissevain, *Saints and Fireworks* (New York: Humanities Press, 1965), chap. 8 and esp. pp. 131–33.
[27] "Protection of Minorities," pp. 338–39.

communalism or racial separation within the large constituency.

The difficulties of list proportionality have already been rehearsed sufficiently; only additional problems found in developing systems are suggested here. First, list proportionality will not work well in states which have existing intercommunal parties. The difficulties of ranking candidates on the list by communities will be a constant source of communal friction that can only lead inevitably to some sort of fractionalization, culminating in separate communal lists in contention. The tendency of the list system of proportional representation to multiply the number of contenders can be far more harmful in a developing state, requiring as it does all the political stability that it can get in the institutions of national policy. Thus, for example, the Indonesian election of 1955 resulted in a legislature in which 250 seats were divided among 22 parties, later to form 17 different parliamentary groups for action in the legislature, although 4 of these parliamentary groups held almost 200 of the seats.[28] Secondly, even if the list system did not open its doors to multiplication of contenders, the absence of strong national parties which are organized to create lists representative of the party as a whole may lead to a situation in which segments of the party find themselves without proper representation on the list of candidates. In short, in the presence of divergent communalism and the absence of strong national organization, list systems of election may cause more difficulties than their advanced techniques of representation may solve.

The real difficulty with both schemes of proportional representation is not in their fractionalization nor in their emphasis upon the national party. Rather, list systems are designed to create a legislature based on numbers and not on social or economic power independent of votes. Thus, in Malaya the adoption of the list system would reward the Malays with about half the legislature, the Chinese with about one-third, the Indians with about one-sixth, roughly equal to their

[28] Herbert Feith, *The Indonesian Elections of 1955* (Ithaca, N.Y.: Cornell University Press, 1957), pp. 87, 88.

voting strength in 1964. Yet vastly underrated would be the
Chinese financial power in favor of the number of Malays, a
situation perilous indeed for a new state. In this connection,
the comment of Herbert Feith about a neighbor state is useful:

> The elections have distributed parliamentary strength in a way
> which does not accord with the reality of effective power rela-
> tionships in Indonesia. They have given parliamentary power
> to the parties, or the leadership of the parties, which were able
> to establish organizational machinery at the level of the village.
> But they leave without parliamentary representation propor-
> tionate to their actual power, and so forced to exert this power
> in extra-parliamentary ways, such groups as the army, the
> Chinese business interests, and the army-veteran-business lead-
> ers of the strong exporting areas in Sumatra and Sulawesi.[29]

Any system of proportional representation is supposed to place
greatest power in the hands of numbers; this emphasis may
be acceptable in a country in which divisions within the state
are relatively severe as long as there is a mass commitment to
the existing economic and social structure. In the developing
state, where one of the primary tasks is the reconciliation of
power relationships with mass voter participation, the effect
of this exclusion of economic power in favor of a pure numerical base for legislative representation creates problems of
stability that are not easily overcome.

Proportional representation in developing states also has its
implications for the legislative body itself. It is certainly op-
timistic to argue that legislatures in developing countries play
a role of importance parallel with that of the legislature in
developed countries. But it is unduly pessimistic to argue that
the legislature in a developing state must only be the formali-
zation and legitimation of communal elites. Whatever the role
— audience for a popular president, constituency service, even
policy decisions — a popularly elected legislature can be a
center of unique political activity, different from either cooperation at the presidential level or informal communication
between social elites in the society at large. Yet proportional

[29] *Ibid.*, p. 91.

representation would seem to produce a legislature whose fissures are those of the society and whose concerns are those of the communal competition in the nation as a whole. Not only would communal issues be carried undiluted in the legislature and thus be given new legitimacy, but issues other than communal ones must either fit some kind of communal mold or be relegated perhaps to the executive or some other policy-making body. A legislature in which elections have not dampened communal strife, in which opposition is more likely to be divided rather than coalescing, in which numbers rather than influence carry weight, makes a poor competitor in the battle to counter the executive.

Of course it can be argued that the mere act of voting is what is important and that the form of the legislature is unimportant. First, as has been noted, this argument assumes an unduly pessimistic attitude toward the legislative body itself. Secondly, if this be the only reason for having elections, it is much more easily done through the simpler process of electing presidents, in any but monarchical regimes. It would seem, however, that an opportunity is lost if legislative elections are not taken seriously. It is in local elections that specific local grievances are aired and the particularism of the developing state may find its expression. It matters little that the legislature will probably not be the agent of change or reform, that indeed it will be the presidential budget or the president's program that takes such local grievances into account. What does matter is the airing of these grievances in local elections as local candidates express the sentiments of local people. Clearly the larger districts required for list proportionality will not fulfill the same function; they may be too heterogeneous, they may have too many unsettled conflicts, indeed they may simply have too many people per representative for any sort of specific identity. It probably matters little if the district is contested under a plurality system; the fact is that a local election provides a local interpretation of national goals and programs, and that can be a salutary experience for an electorate accustomed to edicts from regional administrators of a colonial power.

The legislature produced by proportional representation may indeed serve the purposes of political systems in developing states, but such service may be in spite of proportionality rather than a product of it. The difficulties of the more complex forms of proportionality are such that only the simplest form — the list system — is practicable, and in a multiracial state list proportionality would seem to preserve communalism rather than reduce it as a political force. Furthermore, the implicit assumption of proportionality — that political equality is social equality — might be shared by those communities with small shares of the economic and social pie, but those with relatively larger shares might have grounds for dissatisfaction. In the final analysis, the absence of any prior screening of the contenders for public office other than their coincidence with communal boundaries, places a heavy strain upon the legislature itself, since it must now resolve the controversies in the society which are duplicated in the legislature. There is no form of coalescing, and there is no need for it. The legislature must bear in pure, undiluted form the burdens of the society, and there should be little surprise if the legislature drops them.

CHAPTER VII

Plurality and Coalition
in Developing States

THE MOST DIFFICULT TASK of any nation undergoing change from a traditional society to a modern one is maintaining unity within the society. Whether the stresses be from a drawn out transition period — from agrarian to industrial — or whether they be somewhat abrupt — from colonial to independent state — these strains are of a magnitude only dimly sensed by those in an established state whose social values may occasionally be strained but whose environment as a whole is rarely changed. Indeed, perhaps in the developed state there can be little understanding of the problems of underdevelopment since change in the developed state is slow and rarely punishing for a whole population. The developed state exists with a governmental system whose form may change but whose roles and procedures are established in such a manner that political stability is the expected norm. Parallel with assumed political stability, the direction of the society is established. A developed society has the luxury of knowing who will rule and who will be ruled, who is on the top of the pecking order and who on the bottom. Change occurs but always with reference to these patterns.

The developing society is denied the comfort of clear-cut roles for either the government or the member. In the old society of village or clan or tribe, these expectations were clear, and each member found his own role to play in the system.[1] Any government that might have existed in the territory of the society was an extension of the values of the society; thus, leaders might have strong traditional claims to leadership through religion or tribal membership, if, of course, there were *any* strong multitribe leaders. But traditional society does pass under the influence of forces of modernization and change, altering social patterns through the introduction of city ghettoes rather than village life, and of labor in mines rather than fields, in aluminum smelteries rather than nomadic trading enterprise, in national bureaucracies rather than in traditional village roles. Patterns of government — local and national — that might have existed for centuries also change to forms and techniques that have been imported from abroad and imposed or adopted on local society.[2] It is inevitable that political forms and techniques must change simultaneously with vast social change, although this unhappy coincidence is certainly regrettable.[3]

During this process of change the new nation-state teeters on the edge of disintegration. For one thing, traditional techniques may in form be changed, but the result may be only to increase the sophistication with which old antagonisms may be pursued and vendettas resolved. There is certainly more style in preventive detention of a traditional enemy than there is in the execution of his village compatriots, and the same may be said for the elimination of men as enemies of the state rather than as merely antagonists from another clan.

[1] Cf. Lloyd A. Fallers, *Bantu Bureaucracy* (Chicago: University of Chicago Press, 1965).

[2] For example, the role of opposition uses strategies and tactics that differ with Western forms of political opposition. See, for example, Peter R. Gould, "The Threads of Ghana's Constitution," in Peter R. Gould (ed.), *Africa: Continent of Change* (Belmont, Calif.: Wadsworth Publishing Company, 1961), p. 50.

[3] It is, of course, simply incorrect to assume such changes will be equally difficult for all societies. See, for example, Simon Ottenberg, "Ibo Receptivity to Change," in William R. Bascom and Melville J. Herskovits, *Continuity and Change in African Culture* (Chicago: University of Chicago Press, 1965), pp. 130–43.

Secondly, political control by the new national elite is advanced through the acquisition and employment of new techniques, for example, motor vehicles and radio communication. If nothing more, retaliation against those who dissent may be swifter, although the elements of force may as well be turned against the very government they are supposed to serve. And, of course, the new devices for communication perfected in the developed world are most useful in the dissemination of propaganda, though they may as well be channels of communication through which dissident elements are able to create hostilities beyond the vision of the traditional warrior in the most scenic back country. The advent of modernization brings to leaders the possibilities of national change, yet it gives to those who would seize power or divide the nation equal opportunity to destroy nascent unity.

Through all these possibilities the new nation must work its way, always seeking to do what might have been the impossible for most developed nations in the Western world — build a viable social and economic system, create a stable governing system that is somehow responsive to needs, and at the same time create a sense of national identity. And the time available for all of this is very short. If mass participation in the process of government is desired — and there is no point in discussing elections if it is not — the political system takes on overwhelming importance. First, the party and electoral system must enable the voters to make some sort of meaningful choice about how they feel the elite is governing. Yet this choice must be a restricted one, because the gap between what the elite understands to be important and what the electorate understands may be vast, more so than in developed states. The elite may understand the difficulties of independence and the problems of the social system, while the electorate may be able to see only as far as the local village or at best the local constituency. Secondly, in the act of making a meaningful choice in elections — and this is a most important consideration — the mass population gains a sense of participation in the acts of a new entity, the nation-state. Thus, again the problem of the balance between elite control and national integration emerges to haunt the new state. With these observations in mind it is worth examining two different developing systems. The first is Tanganyika, later to be the mainland part of Tanzania (throughout this discussion the first, and older, name will be used); the second is Malaya, part of the federation of Malaysia (again the older name will be used throughout).

THE NATURE OF THE
PROBLEM IN TANGANYIKA

It is surely true that the Tanganyikan model is not a universal one, for that state had numerous advantages not found in other, less fortunate states seeking independence. First, there was a leader endowed with all the charisma of a successful passage from colony to independence, Dr. Julius Nyerere, Prime Minister and then President under the Republic. Secondly, the independence organization had established credentials as a political party with notable electoral success before independence and with mass acceptance of its role after that date. Thirdly, although racial tensions existed in the colony before independence, they did not immediately become a major concern for the new nation; and tribal animosities were not strong enough to prevent their being absorbed under the umbrella of the national party and leader. Finally, the transition to self-government left few residual hostilities, and these did not substantially affect the operations of the government to follow. In short, the conditions inherited by Dr. Nyerere and his Tanganyika African National Union (TANU) allowed at least some sort of attempt at the dual tasks of nation building and political integration. From an examination of these techniques, perhaps some conclusions can be drawn about this complex problem of emergence.

Tanganyika, later part of Tanzania, moved from protectorate to self-government in 1961, after both German and British colonial regimes, one of many states to make that move in the years between 1955 and 1965. Yet, Tanganyika was different, for Tanganyika accomplished two things that were alien to the British tradition: first, it moved, with some delay, to establish a single-party state as the sole representative party of the whole plural population; and, secondly, it refuted the colonial doctrine — almost dogma — of multiracialism (coexistence coupled with some separation) in East Africa. In the long-term history of Tanganyika these two propositions may far outrank the achievement of republican status, though gained at the same time. Tanganyika accomplished these two feats because it is a plural society in one sense, yet not in another. It has three races: Africans, numbering about 9,000,000; Asians, mainly Indians and Pakistanis, numbering about 72,000; and Europeans, numbering about 21,000.[4] Further, among the Africans there are about 120 tribes, most of them small enough to be safely ignored as individual competitors.[5] So numerous are tribal identities that President Julius Nyerere has on occasion noted that their diversity serves national integration. "The more tribes we have, the better. My own tribe is 35,000 people; my brother is the chief. If my brother wanted to be a nuisance, he couldn't be much of a nuisance." [6] Thus, on the face of it Tanganyika seems the absolute plural society, with different racial groups and the dominant racial group split apart into a number of tribes.

But the dominant racial group is not split apart politically, at least for the time being. The overwhelming African majority is so solidly behind TANU that it was able to demolish all opposition in elections before the advent of the single-party state. President Nyerere noted:

> But it soon became clear to us that, however ready we leaders might have been to accept the theory that an official Opposition was essential to democratic government, our own people thought otherwise; for the idea did not make sense to them. As a result of the people's freely expressed choice at the polls we found ourselves with a one-party system.[7]

[4] Cranford Pratt, "Multi-Racialism and Local Government in Tanganyika," *Race* 2 (November 1960), p. 33.

[5] Margeret L. Bates, "Tanganyika," in Gwendolen M. Carter (ed.), *African One-Party States* (Ithaca, N.Y.: Cornell University Press, 1962), p. 433.

[6] Quoted in J. Clagett Taylor, *The Political Development of Tanganyika* (Stanford, Calif.: Stanford University Press, 1963), p. 96.

[7] "One Party System," *Spearhead* 2 (January 1963), p. 12; See also Republic of Tanzania, *Report of the Presidential Commission on the Establishment of a Democratic One-Party State* (Dar-es-Salaam, 1965), p. 14, par. 32.

The first true expression of the solidarity of the African majority behind the party was witnessed in the separate communal roll elections of 1958–59, in which TANU candidates and TANU endorsed candidates (for the Asian and European reserved seats) [8] swept the boards and destroyed the United Tanganyika Party, the latter committed to the policy of multiracialism. The colonial administration had tried to preserve the idea of communal representation through the use of a common voting roll with seats reserved for each racial group, but the African majority in the common roll exerted its discipline and the concept of the communal franchise was effectively dead. [9]

The seeming success of TANU left it with a momentary dilemma. On the one hand, it was African, and was the African independence movement in opposition to the colonial administration. It had soundly defeated the only party advocating multiracialism, implying commitment to the policy of separate or reserved seats for the different racial blocs. On the other hand, TANU had elected members from all of the races through endorsement, and there were members of all three racial blocs who had actively worked for TANU endorsement and had benefited from the party support. Further, in the 1960 elections TANU won 70 out of 71 seats up for election including seats held by non-Africans. [10] The decision to reject multiracialism had been too successful, for now the country had two different political facts before it: the existence of secured seats for non-Africans, and the political fact of control by the African party. By independence the pattern was established. Tanganyika was to be primarily an African nation dominated by a party oriented toward the African but also toward interracial harmony. The massive African majority had proved too strong for the attempt to preserve communalism in politics. [11]

8 Martin Lowenkopf, "Tanganyika Achieves Responsible Government," *Parliamentary Affairs* 14 (Spring 1961), pp. 245–47.

9 Pratt, "Multi-Racialism," pp. 45–46.

10 The one loss in 1960 was for local rather than communal reasons. Bates, "Tanganyika," p. 430.

11 See Colin Leys, "Tanganyika, the Realities of Independence," *Inter-*

Single-Party Democracy. The trappings of political organization in the republic are not easily understood by those accustomed to traditions of the Western world.[12] First, there is one party, the beneficiary of a constitutional establishment that was expressed in the appendix to the 1964 constitution.[13] Further suggesting the importance of TANU was the genesis of the constitutional linkage, the Presidential Commission on the Establishment of a Democratic One-Party State, whose report became the basis of the close relation between TANU and the state. (Although the report rejected integrating the National Executive Council (NEC) and the National Assembly, it did give to the NEC powers to compel witnesses and to ask for papers.) Secondly, there is the form of presidential election, which is more of a plebiscite than an election and which is almost a mirror copy of the Soviet method of electing members of the Supreme Soviet. Thus, the voter can vote only for the candidate of the party in Tanganyikan presidential elections; the only available alternatives are yes or no. Should the candidate be rejected (President Nyerere won his last election in 1965 by 2,500,000 to 92,000), then the party is empowered to put up another candidate who will again be voted for on a yes or no basis. Finally, no legislative candidate may run without the approval of the NEC of the party and, of course, no person may be a candidate without being a member of the party. In short, the constitution and the party are intertwined,

---

national Journal 17 (Summer 1962), p. 260, for an exposition of the antiminority sentiment among African members of the Assembly. Nyerere's answer is found in *ibid.,* p. 261. An explicit repudiation of the British policy of multiracialism is found in Republic of Tanzania, *Report . . . One-Party State,* p. 13, par. 27.

12 See, for example, Sigmund Neumann, *Modern Political Parties* (Chicago: University of Chicago Press, 1956), p. 395. While Neumann would argue that the single party is inconsistent with democracy, Duverger would argue that the single party, if it succeeds an autocratic rule, may not yet be totally democratic but is certainly a move in that direction. Maurice Duverger, *Political Parties* (London: Methuen & Co., Ltd., 1954), p. 279.

13 A discussion of the linkage of TANU to all phases of Tanganyikan life, as befits a true party of national integration, is found in Harvey Glickman, "One-Party System in Tanganyika," *Annals* 358 (March 1965), pp. 137–49.

the party and the legislature are closely linked, and the party controls access to the powers of government.

But the adage that appearances can be deceiving is no less true here than anywhere else. Although the model seems to sharply resemble that of the Soviet system, and may indeed come to emulate that system more closely, there are sharp distinctions that can be made between the two in all three stages of election to the legislature — nomination, campaign, and election. It is particularly worth concentrating on the legislature, since on occasion it has been somewhat less than cooperative with the charismatic president of the republic while at the same time it has concerns that reflect the constituency representation of any of the modern developed democracies. If the single party has problems with the legislature, or at least must extend itself to control the legislature, then perhaps it is the electoral system that is producing some fissiparous tendencies among the members themselves.

The party in a single-party state must be a truncated affair. It does not have the sense of separateness from other, contending parties that the party models of the developed states possess, but it is not the government either. In the Soviet state, where the party is theoretically open to all those who can gain entrance through the somewhat rigorous procedures, the party is an elite whose sense of responsibility is checked only by the limited role played by the population in the nominating process and by the rational assessment of reality by the members of the party themselves. The party's decisions may indeed be popular and correct for the mass of the population, but the foundation of these decisions is perforce empirical observation by a narrowly based elite rather than the more substantial involvement of a large segment of the society. In Tanganyika, there is a totally different kind of party, a mass party, open to any citizen of the state eighteen years old or over, who puts up the fees and who subscribes "to the principles of TANU as set out in its constitution. . . ." [14] The party begins with a broad base, organized by districts and re-

[14] Republic of Tanzania, *Report . . . One-Party State,* p. 16, par. 38.

gions and culminating in the NEC. From this flows a very important observation: that all candidates must be party members is a much less important thing for Tanganyika than for the Soviet Union simply because the party membership is a mass phenomenon.[15]

The African party is different from the Russian party for another, much more significant, reason, one that profoundly affects the behavior of the party and the attitudes of the population toward it. The parties were drastically affected by the general position in which they found themselves once the period of change to party rule was apparent. While the Bolsheviks could not be sure of power, since the popularity of their revolution was suspect and a consequent rule by an elite was necessary to solidify their power, the pattern was totally different in Tanganyika. TANU had the advantage of being almost totally identified with independence and was the spearpoint of the popular effort to achieve freedom and self-determination. Prior to the institutionalization of the single party in 1965, although TANU, in fact, ruled the state, it competed in a multiparty framework and still won almost all seats in the National Assembly. The allegiance of the people to TANU was real, elections between TANU candidates and independents or other parties were foregone affairs, and the surety of Dr. Nyerere's leadership was an accepted feature of the Tanganyikan landscape.[16] In short, for Tanganyika independence meant freedom through the workings of TANU. Though the voluntary single-party state may be stifling and suppress innovation — the American South for many years is only one example — it still provides a totally different framework from that found in systems where the one party is an imposed elite operating with a narrow base against a sizable

[15] This observation is supported by Colin Legum, "Single Party Democracy?" *World Today* 21 (December 1965), p. 527.

[16] So strong was the hold of TANU on the popular mind that a number of writers argue that the single-party primary system would have the actual effect of opening up the political system. See, for example, William Tordoff, "The General Election in Tanzania," *Journal of Commonwealth Political Studies* 4 (March 1966), p. 47; Lionel Cliffe, "Tanganyika's Two Years of Independence," *Current History* 46 (March 1964), p. 139.

segment of opposition. Perhaps the argument is as well put by Dr. Nyerere as by any other writer:

> Democracy has been described as a "government of the people, by the people, for the people." Surely, if a government is freely elected by the people, there can be nothing undemocratic about it just because nearly all the people, rather than only some of them, happen to have voted it into power. Indeed, it appears natural that young nations which emerge as the result of a nationalist movement having united their people, will be governed at first by a nationalist government as distinct from a party government.[17]

As long as the single party maintains this envious position, there can be little doubt that it can serve both as an integrating symbol for the society and as a ruling party of unrivaled legitimacy.

Because the future development of Tanganyika was identified with TANU, the party's freedom to operate was enhanced substantially. First, since identity with independence meant identity with TANU, the party itself served as a vehicle for the political integration of Tanganyika. There was little immediate need for devices of integration along the lines of the Soviet model — particularly those acts which identified party with state — since this part of the process was already accomplished. Secondly, the party could safely afford to have political competition since the winners would always be associated with the party and dared not risk its ire. The single party maintained its identity as the integrative force of the state and additionally was able to foster competition for legislative office, thus creating a sense of nationhood while at the same time maintaining some control over the ruling elite. Obviously, however, traditional techniques of competition would not suffice, for in the general election there would be no candidate for office other than that put up by TANU itself. The creation of the process required some imagination, although the model was ready at hand: by scrapping the Western idea of a general election between parties, the new format would be instead a variation of the American party primary,

[17] "Will Democracy Work in Africa," in Gould (ed.), *Africa,* p. 53.

in which approved candidates competed in a run-off election and the winner would then be the duly elected member for the constituency.[18]

Organization of the electoral process after the acceptance of this principle was simplicity itself. First, at the constituency level any person could be a candidate who was twenty-one years old, a member of TANU, and who received on a petition the signatures of 25 or more registered voters. The total number of candidates was then forwarded to the party's Special Annual Conference of the District so that preliminary clearance could be provided. At the level of the conference no final decision was made; rather, after each member voted for two of the potential candidates and these votes were tallied, the whole list of names, ranked by the tally of the conference members, was forwarded to the NEC. The NEC was restricted in its choice in that the candidates had to be from the list itself and the NEC had to recommend the top two names on the list unless a majority of the NEC recommended otherwise. The run-off was then held, after a campaign conducted by the District Executive Committee; and the winner became a member of the National Assembly for that constituency. The process is hardly what could be called liberal democracy by Western standards, but it is an effective one for allowing some control within the framework of a one-party state.

There are several tests that can be applied to this particular electoral system to determine if, indeed, it works as well as it seems. First, and simplest, are all candidates given a contest, or is there unanimity around one candidate in each constituency? The data on the September 1965 election, the first under the new system, reveal that there was an extremely large number of candidates: 713 individuals qualified with the requisite number of signatures. In only 6 of the 107 constituencies was there only one candidate put forth from among the electorate,

18 The original report urged that three candidates be nominated for each constituency. Republic of Tanzania, *Report . . . One Party State,* p. 20, par. 56. The proposal was changed in a later document to provide for only two candidates "in order to avoid the possibility of a candidate being elected with minority support." Republic of Tanzania, *Proposals of the Tanzania Government for the Establishment of a Democratic One-Party State* (Dar-es-Salaam, 1965), p. 2.

and in 5 more only two candidates emerged from the constituency.[19] (Among the six single-candidate seats, five were ministers or junior ministers.) Thus, the electorate had the right
to choose its representatives in 101 of the 107 seats, an average
that might indeed be high even in some of the developed
states of the Western world. It should be added that although
in the six constituencies in which there was to be no contest
the electorate was denied a choice in candidates, the party also
had to accept the nominee whether it liked him or not.

A second test is simply how restrictive the party choice is
compared to the preferences of the district conference. Put
another way, how often did the party preference win, and how
often did party officials lose to other candidates. The party
NEC could, it may be recalled, overturn the district conference preference only when one of the top two had poor party
records or when there was a tie for second. In fact, the party
executive exercised a great deal of self-discipline and overturned only sixteen of the district choices by selecting some
potential nominee from further down the list, although in
one case it meant the elimination of party members who were
ministers or were in good standing with the party itself.[20] Thus,
in the nomination process the party remained self-disciplined
even at the cost of some members of the party elite. Did the
electorate support the party's choices? No less than 44 of the
party's first choices went down to defeat in 101 contested constituencies, including the then Minister for Finance, beaten by
a farmer from the constituency. Thus, in slightly less than
half the cases the first choice of the district conference of party
members was defeated, and the electorate was able to impose
its will even within this somewhat limited framework.[21]

Finally, how much did the party intervene to defeat candidates it did not want and to further the fortune of candidates

[19] Belle Harris, "The Tanzanian Elections," *Mbioni* 2 (no. 5), p. 10(?).
[20] Legum, "Single Party Democracy?" p. 528.
[21] Casualties on the Government (or really party) side were impressive.
Of the 31 sitting members who survived the nominating process, 16 were
beaten; of the 31 TANU officeholders nominated, 22 were unsuccessful.
Harris, "Elections," p. 24(?).

in good standing? First, there are a large number of rules governing the behavior of candidates, particularly with reference to the role of the party or the President. Thus, no candidate is able to claim the personal endorsement of the President or of the party. The official line is, in fact, the opposite. All candidates are considered equally acceptable to the party and to the President, to the extent that the party gives each candidate the same resources for campaigning. Further, a three-man commission from another constituency oversees each election to ensure that no endorsement is claimed and that the campaign resources of each candidate are approximately the same. As a catalog for fair elections, there are few systems that will match the Tanganyikan, as described by Colin Legum:

> No candidate is allowed to spend personal funds in the election; the Party provides all the facilities for an election campaign. The candidates must appear together at all meetings which are arranged by the Party; they alternate in speaking first. They must travel from meeting to meeting in the same car, again provided by the Party. Their printed election appeal is confined to a single manifesto (produced by the Party) in which each candidate is allowed a page to state his qualifications in any terms he chooses.[22]

The effectiveness of the system, and perhaps a testament to its fairness, is evident in the results of the September 1965 election: "the defeat of two Ministers, two former Ministers, six prominent junior Ministers, a dozen important holders of public office, and other Party stalwarts." [23] It is doubtful that the party would have allowed such a sudden turnover in the elite if it had felt itself able to intervene, so that it is not out of line to conclude that the 1965 election was run according to the standards of fairness laid down in the electoral rules.

The Tanganyikan election system provides for the two variables with which all election systems must be concerned, integration of the population (through representation) and the

---

[22] "Single Party Democracy?" p. 529.
[23] *Ibid.*, p. 530.

control of the elite. The plebiscite for presidential election has many of the overtones of the Soviet model, complete with the "yea or nay" format that in reality becomes something of an endorsement for the national elite as well as the focus upon the one man who then becomes the embodiment of the regime. On the other hand, the legislative electoral system is much more a device for registering local dissatisfaction with the policies of the government and the skill with which local parliamentarians are able to handle constituency demands. Through the single-member district and competition within the framework of the one party, voters achieve a sense of control and a sense of representation, while legislative stability is maximized.[24] Integration and stability are achieved, however, at the cost of severe limitations on party competition; and were TANU and President Nyerere not the heroic figures that they are, the democratic aspects of the single-party state might be sorely tried.[25] In an attempt to achieve integration and stability in a more democratic framework — in part dictated by the absence of a charismatic leader and heroic party — other multiracial states have adopted different techniques. One such state is Malaya (now part of Malaysia) in which an attempt has been made to combine multiracial partnership in one party while maintaining the freedom to create opposing parties based around interests not benefiting from racial alliance.

THE NATURE OF THE
PROBLEM IN MALAYA (1952–1966)

Since the primary difficulties created by techniques that emphasize group representation — proportional systems, or tech-

[24] Belle Harris argues that two of the three general propositions that emerge from a study of the election are manifestations of localism: the issues were local and the voters chose men who could most effectively represent local interests. "Elections," p. 25(?).

[25] The observation of Martin Lowenkopf is worth noting: the proof of TANU's "commitment to parliamentary democracy will best be seen in the tribute it pays to the democratic parliamentarian 'cloak,' i.e., in the degree of opposition to policy, not just technical detail, the Government allows from the backbench — and the number of purges, and their causes, the party makes." "Tanganyika Achieves Responsible Government," p. 257.

niques whereby groups are guaranteed their own representatives in legislatures — are such that communalism is continued rather than diminished, other techniques of election are in the long run more advantageous to the pluralist political system. The goals sought by a noncommunal electoral system seem evident: first, the preservation of communal politics should not be an immediate by-product; secondly, some form of stable legislative majority must be formed as a result of restrictions built into the electoral system; and finally, and most importantly, significant communal groups must each have a fair share of the representation, although there is now a new meaning for the word "fair," in which precise proportion is only one part. Proportional techniques that require mass literacy are obviously out, and the list system, which does not, is not acceptable because it tends to develop communal contenders. Thus, the technical requirements are relatively clear: a plurality system, incorporating coalition-building techniques which will hopefully force together divergent groups not willing to cooperate under proportional or other communal-oriented systems of election, although there obviously must be some minimal willingness to cooperate, even with some reluctance. Fortunately, there is at hand the Alliance party of the Federation of Malaysia (for convenience we examine here only the federated states of Malaya proper).

There Are Migrants and There Are Migrants. The demography of Malaya is of particular importance to the study of politics in that country for it is the basis of the Alliance party technique and at the same time it raises questions about the exportability of the model. First, the eleven states composing the Malay Federation are not totally Malay in ethnic origin, nor are the Malays even numerically dominant in the federation. Rather, the country is a nation of migrants.[26] Aborigines and the immigrant Malays shared the country during the early nineteenth century, the former playing the role of Aborigines everywhere — Indians, Bushman, or Maoris — grad-

---

[26] See T. H. Silcock, "Communal and Party Structure," in T. H. Silcock and E. K. Fisk, *The Political Economy of Independent Malaya* (Canberra: Australian National University, 1963), pp. 1–27, *passim*.

ually fading from importance while the latter became a nucleus
for migration from Indonesia later in the century. The second
wave of migration featured Chinese and Indians: the first
were brought in to work the tin mines and to establish rudimentary commercial enterprise while the second came in
smaller numbers for exploitation of Malaya's second great natural resource, rubber. Thus an initial pattern was established:
the Malays came into the country first, adopting agriculture
and coastal fishing which were not directly concerned with
money economy but were based upon a family settlement pattern; [27] and then came the Chinese and Indians, both of whom
entered the country on a contract basis for the exploitation
of natural resources in return for wages, not apparently for
settling into the country in any permanent sense.[28] Not until
the middle of the twentieth century do the Chinese and Indians adopt a permanent settlement pattern.

In addition to apparent impermanence of attachment to the
land, non-Malays differed in other ways. While the Malays
by and large could claim to speak the same language (though
this may not really be so), most definitely Indians and Chinese
were not conversant with the language. Although the non-
Malay peoples might not be able to communicate save in
English, there seems to have been little effort to learn Malay
beyond that amount needed for commercial and official transactions. Speaking a different language is one thing that in
time might be overcome,[29] but the dedication of the Malay to

[27] The importance and advantages of a money orientation are stressed in
Maurice Freedman, "The Handling of Money," *Man* 59 (April 1959),
art. 89.

[28] Soh Eng Lim notes, "The Chinese came to Malaya mainly to earn a
livelihood or to amass wealth, . . . most of them were transients in
Malaya." "Tan Cheng Lock: His Leadership of the Malayan Chinese,"
Journal of Southeast Asian History 1 (March 1960), p. 35. See also Chan
Heng Chee, "The Malayan Chinese Association" (unpublished Masters
thesis, University of Singapore, 1965), pp. 4–5.

[29] See Gerald P. Dartford, "Malaya: Problems of a Polyglot Society,"
Current History 34 (June 1958), pp. 246–351, for a general discussion of
the background of Malaya, emphasizing the language difficulties. See also
Margaret Roff, "The Malayan Chinese Association," *Journal of Southeast
Asian History* 6 (September 1965), pp. 40–53, *passim,* for a discussion from
the Chinese prespective. The difficulties presented by education in a
minority language are explored in Wolfgang Franke, "Chinese into Ma-
laysians," *Far Eastern Economic Review* 47 (March 12, 1965), pp. 459–61.

the religion of Islam is quite another thing, and the aim of the Pan-Malayan Islamic Party for a Muslim theocratic state might leave the non-Malay apprehensive if not distrustful. Finally, the pattern of settlement of the various communities is a factor worth noting: the Malays by and large are found in the rural parts of the country, the non-Malays in the urban areas or at least in the parts of the country where there are urban-oriented business establishments, such as mining or large estates. The logical extension of settlement patterns is found in the domination of some of the states by Malays, notably those in the north where Malay concentration is 90 percent of the population, while in other states, such as Selangor on the west coast, the proportion of Chinese is more than half.[30]

To sum up, the patterns of immigration and settlement brought about population distributions that were enhanced by cultural and religious differences and by an apparent difference in nationalist attachment to the country. As two authors quite familiar with the Malayan scene have suggested:

> The Malays also have cultural advantages. . . . The Chinese, on the other hand, are in control of practically all trade and commerce with the exception of what is under foreign (mainly British) control.[31]

Malays may have had the culture on their side, but the Chinese had the money.

Until recently the Malay had more than culture on his side; he had votes. At the census of 1957 the Malays made up about 50 percent of the population, the Chinese about 37 percent, and the Indians about 11 percent.[32] While there was no restriction on Chinese citizenship in the original constitution,[33]

[30] T. E. Smith, "The Malayan Elections of 1959," *Pacific Affairs* 33 (March 1960), p. 41. See also Maurice Freedman, "The Growth of a Plural Society in Malaya," *Pacific Affairs* 33 (June 1960), pp. 158–68.

[31] R. S. Milne and K. J. Ratnam, "Politics and Finance in Malaya," *Journal of Commonwealth Political Studies* 3 (November 1965), p. 183.

[32] Gordon P. Means, "Malaysia — A New Federation in Southeast Asia," *Pacific Affairs* 36 (Summer 1963), p. 140.

[33] "The Chinese were brought in as a result of foreign rule, with which they had collaborated to their own advantage and to the disadvantage of the Malays, until the Malays achieved independence." Silcock, "Communal and Party Structure," p. 5.

the Malays seem to presume that the Chinese are still transients. Particularly after 1957, the Chinese lost the right to a
very simplified form of citizenship, mere registration.[34] As of
1962 even long-resident Chinese were forced to seek naturalization, although any Chinese born in Malaya is of course automatically a citizen. As a result of this rather complex tangle
of citizenship clauses in the constitution, the Malays began
independence with a rather sizable edge in number of electors,
far above that expected from their numbers. Thus, for the
1955 election it has been estimated that the electorate was 84
percent Malay and about 11 percent Chinese, although a citizenship and registration drive sharply cut the Malay margin
to only about 57 percent of the electorate in 1959.[35] Should
this trend continue, and there is little reason to doubt that it
will, one observer has estimated that within a generation the
states of the federation that elect two-thirds of the parliament
will be a majority non-Malay.[36]

Perhaps the social and economic patterns that form the
basis of Malayan electoral politics can now be seen in perspective. First, no community can effectively dominate the system
through its numbers, for no community has a majority nor
does any community have enough in common with any other
to join in some effort against the third. Second, there is a pre-
ponderance of wealth and economic skill in one community,
the Chinese, although that community does not have nearly
the population to support political domination in a democratic
framework. Finally, while social and economic cleavages are
important, there are other off-setting loyalties that cut across
lines and prevent one community from confronting another.[37]

[34] In fact, citizenship by the doctrine of *jus soli* was something of a
victory for the Chinese association. Soh Eng Lim, "Tan Cheng Lock,"
p. 54; Roff, "Malayan Chinese Association," p. 44.

[35] K. Turner, "Some Comments on the 1964 Malayan Elections," *Australian Outlook* 19 (April 1965), p. 64.

[36] Silcock, "Communal and Party Structure," pp. 16–17.

[37] For example, there seems no direct competition between communities
for civil service positions, and as late as 1962 the positions of the service
(as opposed to technical and professional) seemed to be generally Malay
occupied. Robert O. Tilman, *Bureaucratic Transition in Malaya* (Durham,
N.C.: Duke University 1964), pp. 68–76. How long the service can remain
free of communal competition is of course a matter for conjecture.

In crude form, the Chinese have economic power but for the moment the Malays have the political power. This generalization was especially true in the beginning, in the formation of the Alliance party.

The Alliance in Action. In a pluralist system such as that in Malaya, there are two possible roads for a competitive party system to travel in the absence of formal protections for minorities. First, the parties might be organized around ethnic communities. Thus, there might have developed in the federation a party for the Malays, one for the Chinese, and one for the Indians, with several very minor parties revolving around groups too small to gain stature as national competitors. For this development there would have to be at least three preconditions, aside from any considerations of social stability or potential coalitioning: first, that there is a coincidence of powers, economic, social, and political; second, that no one community have sufficient strength to gain a majority of the electorate and run the country in its own interest; and third, that there be some geographic separation of the communities so that the single-member district system might easily work its way, preventing a heavy concentration of one community (such as the northern Malays in Kelantan and Trengganu) from "wasting" its votes in support of one community party while more evenly distributed communities (such as the Chinese) waltz into power on a series of plurality victories. In actual fact, none of these preconditions was met in Malayan politics at the time of the 1955 elections, and the result was overwhelming political pressure toward another format.

That format is the Alliance party. Simply enough, the communal parties of the three groups — the United Malay National Organization, the Malayan Chinese Association, and the Malayan Indian Congress — agreed to unite into one political organization that would be the major focus of the political activities of the three communities, although the party system would still be competitive.[38] Compared to a single-party state attempting to do the same thing, of course, there are certain

---

[38] The origins of the Alliance are found in the municipal elections of Kuala Lumpur, 1952, apparently without the consent of the Chinese leadership. Soh Eng Lim, "Tan Cheng Lock," p. 56.

problems. First, there is the obvious threat from one communal party to go its own way on the real or imagined assumption that there is greater profit in separate communal politics. The invitation to separate is always present in a competitive situation compared to the situation in which only one party is allowed to contest elections, such as the African state of Tanganyika. The second threat, potentially much more important, is the emergence of issues that cross-cut class or regionalism and might be the base for parties of noncommunal orientation. Thus, for example, in the Malayan case the existence of a radical party or a party of leftist orientation is always possible, especially given the orientation of the Alliance party toward wealthy Chinese and away from the Chinese laborer in the tin mine or in cities. Thus, on the one hand, the growth to excess of the communalism that made the party possible might destroy it; or the emergence of noncommunal issues might also create havoc in the Alliance.

Basic to the Alliance party concept are two operating principles. First, the communities must somehow through their leadership work out the patterns of nomination so that each community receives equal shares. And integral to the distribution of nominees is the second principle, that of providing votes. On the basis of community population, given that Malays made up approximately half of the total population in 1957, that proportion of candidates should as well be Malay. But, since at that time more than half of the electorate was Malay, and thus presumably more than half of the party's votes might be from that community, then perhaps the Malays should receive a higher proportion of the candidates. In fact, the basic distributive principle for the Alliance has been votes, as Table VII.1 illustrates. The minimal increase in the Chinese

TABLE VII.1[a]

	Total seats	Malay	Chinese	Indian
1955	52	35	15	2
1959	104	70	31	3
1964	104	68	33	3

[a]From R. K. Vasil, "The 1964 General Election in Malaya," *International Studies* 7 (1965–66), pp. 60–61.

share from the beginning — still undervalued because the Chinese share of the vote is greater than the percentage of candidates — reflects poorly the increasing share of Chinese electors and the relatively decreasing share of Malays. In fact, in 1959 there were several Chinese resignations from the Malayan Chinese Association (MCA) on the grounds that the Chinese share of candidates was insufficient in light of the increasing Chinese representation in the general electorate.[39]

Though the Alliance was spectacularly successful in its first three elections, it has not fought unopposed; and opposition has developed from two different sources: Malay nationalists who believe that the Alliance is not serving Malay interests, and issue-oriented left parties, which are still attempting to woo Chinese voters away from the Alliance. Perhaps the most immediate competition is the Pan-Malayan Islamic Party (PMIP), a strongly pro-Malay party with its strength since 1955 concentrated in the two most isolated yet most heavily Malay states of Kelantan and Trengganu. PMIP is the model communal party, advocating in the 1950s the establishment of Islam as the state religion, the elimination of preference or even first-class citizenship for non-Malays, and the maintenance of Malay as the official language. While it has represented the most constant threat to the alliance system of the federation, it operates against considerable odds: first, the Malays have not been a majority of the population and their share of the electorate is declining although not their share of the total population; secondly, many of the party's original demands have been met, particularly with regard to language, religion, and Chinese citizenship, and the implementation of more extreme demands might lead to significant Chinese dissent. Thus, the threat from the Malay side of communalism is less than might be expected, although it is always a force with which the federation must reckon.[40]

The threat from the opposite side of the communal system,

---

[39] Roff, "Malayan Chinese Association," p. 52, notes that Chinese voters do not support the Alliance to the extent that Malays do; see also K. G. Tregonning, "Malaya, 1959," *Australian Quarterly* 32 (June 1960), pp. 41–43, who cites particularly urban defections in the elections of 1959.

[40] Compare T. E. Smith, "Malayan Elections," pp. 46–47.

the Chinese voters, is perhaps more important. First, there are emerging serious problems in the economy of Malaya, especially as synthetics replace world consumption of primary Malayan exports, tin and rubber. Secondly, the Chinese leadership has in the past been more than generous to the Malay leadership on such crucial questions as naturalization and power within the party. Thirdly, the Chinese leadership may be less than inspiring to young Chinese perhaps in search of a more interesting government than one that pragmatically balances communal demands with commercial interests.[41] But while the opportunity for political gain among the urban Chinese exists, there have been problems in implementing a political challenge to the Alliance. No less than four parties successfully appealed to the Chinese voters in 1964, and the lack of an organized opposition in a single-member constituency system of course favors the largest party in the state. Malaya is no exception; and in the 1964 elections, although the Alliance won only about 57 percent of the vote, it won 89 of 104 seats in the federal parliament. Thus, with an opposition divided not only in approach but then divided again within each of the two approaches, the Alliance has been able to dominate Malayan politics for the past decade and more.[42]

The actual performance of the Alliance in elections suggests that its total success is a result of a series of partial successes. For example, while each of the three dominant communities contribute candidates, all the candidates from one single bloc have never been successful in the election. In the 1959 general election there were 74 Alliance candidates elected out of a possible 104. Had all 70 of the Malay candidates been elected and all 3 Indian candidates, there would have been only 1 Chinese sitting on the Alliance benches. In fact, nothing of the kind occurred, since only 52 of the Malay candidates won, 3 of the Indians were successful, and 19 of the Chinese. The partial success of the different communal nominees made the

---

[41] R. S. Milne, "Malaysia," *Asian Survey* 4 (February 1964), p. 700.

[42] The fact that in 1964 only eight Alliance seats were won on plurality might be attributed to the lack of a clear voter alternative rather than to strength of the Alliance. Cf. Turner, "1964 Malaysia Elections," pp. 69–71.

whole system a bit more balanced. A second partial success is the imperfect mobilization of communities. If the Malays had supported the Alliance wholeheartedly and the Chinese only partially, there would be some grounds for suggesting that the party was on weak foundations; but only parts of each community supported the party. Allusion has already been made to Chinese defection, but Malay defection is also important. The two states with the heaviest concentration of Malays and at the same time with a history of strong support for Malay nationalism have generally decided to forego support for the Alliance in favor of the PMIP. While this has given the Malay nationalists seats in Parliament, it has also weakened their influence in the Alliance party since there are obviously fewer Malays supporting the Alliance. Finally, lest the Malays come up too short in their influence within the party, there is a deliberate malapportionment factor which allows the Malay-dominated rural areas to have more representation than the non-Malay urban areas.[43] Thus, it can be argued that the Alliance owed its great strength in Malayan politics to partial success of communal blocs of nominees, imperfect mobilization of communal voting blocs, and a mild gerrymander of the districts. It is equally plausible to argue that these factors contributed to the internal stability of the party.

Preconditions for Alliance. The Alliance party has apparently served Malaya, a multiracial state, as the requisite institution for the integration of economic power and voting power, held in different hands. The necessity for this integration is obvious, for as one student has put it:

> If, in a plural society where racial groups distrust each other, there is a gross lack of balance between the representation each group receives and the power which each has outside the legislature, the hostility of the "under-represented" may threaten the whole system.[44]

While "distrust" is perhaps too mild a term for the Malayan

43 Silcock, "Communal and Party Structure," p. 17, n. 32.
44 Pratt, "Multiracialism," p. 37.

context, the proposition is still true in light of the observation that less than two-fifths of the population controlled well over three-fifths of the financial resources.[45] Seen in that light, the necessity of some form of integrating political device became paramount, and the form that developed was the Alliance party.

As a substitute for more formal minority protective devices — communal rolls or reserved seats or even proportional representation — the Alliance party has a great deal to be said for it. First, and perhaps most important, formal political activity takes place after communal sensitivities have been dealt with, which gave Malaya the advantage of a legislature and government able to move beyond communal concerns. The Alliance party at its most effective was a buffer between the legislature and the communal tensions which might cause severe strains to the system of government. Secondly, a tradition of informal bargaining develops between communities that might otherwise never meet except on the legislative floor.[46] Certainly, the myriad number of agreements that are struck between communal leaders over nominees, and which constituencies which nominees are to fight, and even which cabinet portfolios are to be held by which communities, are all valuable experiences for the leaders of potentially disruptive communities. Finally, for the electorate there is the experience of casting its vote for the party of its choice — regardless of which community the candidate represents — rather than for some narrower interest or community. The Alliance party therefore seems to be one formula for the wedding of the stability of the single-member district system with the national integration necessary in a plural society. Why, then, is it a technique not found more often in the underdeveloped

45 Silcock, "Communal and Party Structure," p. 3.

46 Harvey Stockwin has noted, "Visitors to Malaya often equate the absence of too much free speaking with the preventive detention laws; the absence is more the result of an instinctive preference for quiet compromise and accommodation, for the avoidance of frank and open discussion of divergent opinions, especially communal ones. Such clarification of the issues is seen by Kuala Lumpur as a likely prelude to discord. . . ." "A House Divided," *Far Eastern Economic Review* 47 (March 4, 1965), p. 372.

world? In short, it requires a number of preconditions simply not found elsewhere. The Alliance is a party of consensus existing among a number of parties that influence the majority coalition yet are themselves beyond the margins of the consensus.

> Outside the margin are several opposition groups and parties, dissident groups from the ruling party, and other interest groups and important individuals. These groups outside the margin do not constitute alternatives to the ruling party. Their role is to constantly pressurize, criticize, censure and influence it by influencing opinion and interests inside the margin and, above all, exert a latent threat that if the ruling group strays away too far from the balance of effective public opinion, and if the factional system within it is not mobilized to restore the balance, it will be displaced from power by the opposition groups.[47]

Necessarily, maintaining consensus and factional balance within the dominant party requires a set of circumstances not normally found in the developing world. First, and most obvious, there must be something that each group can contribute to the success of the whole; thus the Chinese in Malaya contributed the financial resources to support the Alliance. Secondly, no group can predominate in the population. While economic power is important, if the vast majority of the population is of another community, then indeed it might be difficult to maintain the delicate balances required for the Alliance party. Thirdly, there should be a relatively peaceful history of relations between the communities, a variable not found in every country.[48] The comparison with South Africa might be suggested, where the failure of two communities to

---

[47] While Kothari is here speaking of India, the parallel to Malaya is perhaps not out of order. Rajni Kothari, "The Congress System in India," *Asian Survey* 4 (December 1964), p. 1162.

[48] Of course, Malaya has not had a completely peaceful history of communal relations either. Serious communal conflicts after the war, for example, fostered the drive for Malay security forces. See Ishak bin Tadin, "Dato Onn and Malay Nationalism," *Journal of Southeast Asian History* 1 (March 1960), p. 65. The riots after the election of 1969 and the apparent refusal of the Chinese party to cooperate with the Alliance government would seem to cast a very dark shadow over the future of communal relations and of the alliance system.

cooperate is in large part due to the enmities generated by the Jameson Raid and the Boer War. Fourthly, the partial intermingling of all different communities geographically creates a climate within which intercommunal compromise is possible. Finally, and perhaps as important as the first precondition, the Alliance in Malaya had the nationalist mystique, for it had guided Malaya from pluralist colony to independent, interracial federation and thus was identified with the birth of the nation-state, an advantage denied other contending parties. Some or most of these advantages are found elsewhere, but the proper coincidence occurred in Malaya in the early 1950s.

SUMMARY AND COMMENT

The two new states examined here — each with similar developmental problems but different social systems — developed a different form of political system to deal with their post-independence problems. In both Malaya and Tanganyika a primary issue was the relations between the racial communities: how the different communities would live together after the country became independent, or whether the country would suffer from a primitive blood bath that would set back not only its own independence but that of every potentially independent plural society. In these societies there were two clearly defined stages in the process of establishing a government: first, party and electoral systems had to be developed that could reconcile the potentially disruptive power imbalances among the communities, in short, there had to be reconciliations at the structural stage; and secondly, there was the actual interaction of communal interests through these structures, that is, the aggregation stage. Until the structural stage is completed — and it will never be completed perfectly, there will always be difficulties — the second stage of aggregation becomes a matter more or less for academic discussion. In the two states considered here, the natures of the social systems dictated a different resolution of the structural stage, although each went through a form of multiracialism, that is, separate identity with guaranteed representation for competing communal groups. In Tanganyika multiracialism took the form of communal seats in the preindependence period; in Malaya it took the form of communal parties such as the PMIP or the Party Negara of Dato Onn. In each case multiracialism was rejected, and different versions of interracialism — cooperation through institutions with representation the result of informal negotiations — came to dominate the structural stage.

The nature and extent of interracialism in the two countries was in part due to the distribution of communities. In Tanganyika the sheer volume of the African vote — representing a majority in every constituency even on a restricted suffrage such as that in 1960 — made the concept of alliance impractical. Yet the accumulation of social and economic power, not to mention European international influence, of the two minority races necessitated some concessions in that direction, accomplished by a commitment (apparently only temporary) to an interracial nation with a small number of candidates selected from the minority communities. In Malaya, however, since no one community predominated, the commitment to interracialism was forced one step further. Instead of merely having some candidates from all communities somewhere in the nation, a rough proportional distribution of these candidates was decided on before the election took place. Thus, the degree and extent of interracial commitment in the structural stage became a function of the size of the dominant group; the degree of minority representation was determined by their power outside the legislative process.

The impact of these resolutions of the structural stage is found in the actual working of the second, the aggregation, stage. In each state there has been a commitment to competition, not so much on theoretical as on practical grounds. Simply enough, the existence in Tanganyika of one dominant racial community whose demands are relatively consistent, who are united behind independence, leader, and party, made the one-party state possible. Within the one-party state there exists a technique for the expression of local dissatisfactions and for local needs — the primary — that provides the necessary outlet for any separatist tendencies that might be engendered. In Malaya the problem was much more complex. Within each of the three communities there might have been a reasonable degree of unity on goals and demands, but bringing the three communities into the one party demanded too much compromise. The one party was not able to handle the demands of all sections of all three groups with nearly the facility that the single party was able to handle one race in Tanganyika, and as a result multipartyism became the order of the day in Malaya. In each case the party supposedly represents about the same proportion of the state, but in Tanganyika that base community is roughly homogeneous, in Malaya it is composed of three distinct communities in a momentary truce. In Malaya, both the nomination process and the electoral process are necessary for the representation of diverse interests.

These two cases are examples of new nations attempting to bring together the institutional form of the single-member district system of elections and the plural society. As said before, the basic problems are in two stages: first, some structural reconciliation of the communal difficulties, and then aggregation of particular local or regional concerns. In Tanganyika, the majority held by one race allowed for a one-party system with only a commitment to interracialism; in Malaya, the distribution of numbers among the communities forced a formal commitment to interracialism and a multiparty system, with the Alliance party only dominant and not exclusive. The systems each performed their primary functions well, at least for a while: they reduced tensions among the communities and allowed the expression of local dissatisfactions while at the same time producing relatively stable legislatures and governments that could engage in legislative activity beyond the mere reconciliation of contending communal blocs. In short, in each case through the use of preelection techniques the party became the instrument for national integration, leaving the legislature free to concentrate on national problems. For the moment, each state developed a workable solution to the problems presented by popular electoral participation in plural societies.

ELECTORAL SYSTEMS IN PLURAL
SOCIETIES: AN EVALUATION

Perhaps the most debatable feature of the various electoral devices used to represent different cultural groups in plural societies is the emphasis on pure representation of numbers rather than upon the representation of the realities of social power. Put another way, the problems presented by pure representation and power representation are the expectations implicit in the schema of representation. The devices of separate electoral rolls for communal groups, or even the Ceylonese "honest gerrymander" (deliberate malapportionment favoring minority groups), assume that from separate representation will flow the protection that each minority desires and, further, that the minority will utilize this representation to gain communal goals. Thus, power relationships are fixed in formal — that is, legally identifiable — group terms, and the outcome is equally fixed. If the minority is apathetic, or if it is aggressive, there is no difference in its representation, and there is no way to increase or decrease its numerical influence in the legislature. The emphasis on representation focuses the attention of group leadership upon the formal act of being represented rather than upon the use to which this representation may be put. The fluidity characteristic of an alliance party within a single-member district electoral system allows the realities of power to find ways of expression, and the aggressive minority may indeed maximize its influence to the detriment of a more apathetic majority. But if the relationships between minorities are fixed by law, then indeed the influences of cultural groups within the political system are static, and there is little effort to go beyond a minimally representative elite which may still be dominated by the majority group.

But here a caveat must be introduced. While the alliance party system may be the long-run salvation of any plural society, and indeed is probably the goal of more enlightened members of the ruling elite, it is not always possible to bury the hostilities among members of the society so easily. It is obvious that the essential precondition for success is relative freedom from intense group hostilities. However, since the alliance system allows the aggressive minority freedom to exert influence, either in terms of candidates or issues, there is always the grave danger that minority activities will create within the majority electorate a reaction against the minority and the coalition leadership which brought it to power. When this occurs, communal harmony no longer exists, and the alliance concept becomes obsolete. Majority politicians must reject the minority in order to save their own power positions, and the minority may indeed find that it has become an object of general hostility, excluded from the political system, and an object of social attack.

The debate between pure representation and power representation is only a variation of the debate between proportional and plurality electoral systems: whether to allot representation to formally recognized groups in the society, which then resolve their differences in the legislative assembly, or whether to allow each group to work out its power base as best it can in the society and then have that series of resolutions reflected in the legislative assembly. In the one case the hope for political integration lies with a multiple legislature, composed of a number of competing groups; in the other case, hope lies in the integrative effects of the party system, with the legislature more often policy maker than social integrator. By perceiving problems of electoral representation in these terms the comparability of developing and developed electoral systems is clearer, for the variables expressed are those of representation and stability, cohesion and fractionalization.

In each case, developed or not, the problem of representation is the same. How much weight should be given to pure numbers of voters versus how much weight should be given to the ability of interests to forge significant coalitions? In the highly cohesive society the problem is not grave. There are not large numbers of divergent groups, and the general path of policy is laid down in advance of government action by the processes of aggregation. In modest form this observation even applies to the two cases of Tanganyika and Malaya. But in the rigidly noncohesive society the problem is quite different, for here the basis of any form of prelegislative coalition is most likely absent. In such societies a plurality electoral system may indeed result in the domination by one large group which has little in common with other groups, unprotected by the non-proportional aspects of plurality. Since there is no distinct pattern of national policy within which the new government must operate, the change of policy will at best be capricious, at worst destructive to the whole system. Thus, some form of broad and guaranteed representation is necessary — in developing states it is separate rolls or reserved seats, in developed states it is proportional representation. In any case the essential prerequisite to successful government in noncohesive societies is the resolution of the dilemma of representation.

Only when the problem of adequate representation is solved may concern for legislative stability become paramount. In a very real sense, legislative stability is a luxury, available only in those systems which have overcome the separatist tendencies of minority groups and which can now express the will of the electorate through a disciplined electoral system. Once it has been established that electoral victory is the result of cooperation within a national system rather than outside of it, then limitations can be placed upon the number of competitors who can achieve representation, either through restrictive devices on size of majority or by a change in the form of election so that in fact the number of victors is limited, hopefully to a majority party or coalition and one or a few opposition parties. Thus, the development of an electoral system that will provide adequate representation for the level of social cohesion which the society has attained is an essential first step on the way to a sound representative democracy.

Obviously, from the discussion here, developing societies have greater difficulties than do modern states in creating an adequate system of representation. A developed state may at least be able to bank upon some sense of national identity that will force stability in times of crisis; a developing state may or may not have such a sense of national identity. A de-

veloped state may at least be able to depend upon a modest
degree of politicization among its electors, even if it is only an
understanding of the nature of mass political participation;
the electorate in a developing state may be casting its collec-
tive vote for the first time. As a minimum, the developed state
will have a literate electorate which will be able to handle the
difficulties of complex electoral devices usually associated with
modified proportional representation systems; the developing
state may have a large illiterate population able to vote only
by symbol or voice and not able to comprehend the sophistication of the single transferable vote or even some modifications
of list proportionality. In order to preserve some form of
minority protection and at the same time maintain the essential simplicity required for an inexperienced electorate, developing states may be forced to resort to artificial rolls or
reserved seats as the only form which can produce adequate
representation without the by-product of a hopelessly confused electorate unable to utilize its own electoral system.

CHAPTER VIII

Conclusion

IN THIS FINAL CHAPTER some tentative conclusions are drawn about the relationship between electoral systems and their environment and about the problems of representation through techniques of election. Perhaps in this manner the volume may be summarized while at the same time some of the questions proposed in the text will be clarified.

1. Two propositions immediately come to mind about the impact of proportional representation and plurality upon government stability and popular representation. Because proportional representation, particularly the list system, tends to emphasize representation more than stability of the governing coalition, other things being equal, there will be a larger number of parties represented in the legislature than would be the case under plurality and the governmental coalition will therefore be more difficult to maintain. Under proportionality it is obviously more difficult to mold a policy coalition that will persist over time with sufficient strength to hold a steady and constant line of policy. If the electoral system tends to build into the processes of government patterns of instability, particularly if the electoral system cannot prevent the emergence of potentially destructive issues in the upper levels of the government, such as linguistic or religious conflicts in legislature or cabinet, elections come to have very clear implications for the complex processes of economic and

political development. Less clear is the implication of short-term instability in the face of powerful internal change, perhaps exemplified by the emergence of social homogeneity in Western Europe since the Second World War. It is precisely in this area, where the forging of a coalition for long-term governing is important, that proportionality, with its emphasis upon the immediate representation of differences in the society, is so likely to cause major difficulties. In relatively stable societies it is of less consequence, but in periods of significant social change proportional representation may fail the social system by not providing a stable political coalition powerful enough to weather the social challenge.

2. If the effect of proportional representation is to place obstacles in the path of stable governing coalitions, it is of course even more effective in dispersing the party structure of opposition. Since proportionality creates a number of parties with little inclination to reduce their numbers down to two, there is an inevitable tendency for the larger parties to form together a government coalition at least temporarily in power. Since it is obviously a simpler process to build a governing majority out of larger parties rather than smaller, the opposition is often reduced to a cluster of smaller parties unable to cooperate during elections and now left to cooperate in the legislature, united by little more than their dislike of the government in power. And even then the opposition is not cemented by a realistic hope that it is an alternative to the government in power, for at best a given minor party might hope to be an ally of some larger party asked to form a new coalition, but the more likely prospect is for the large parties in the defeated coalition to widen the spectrum just enough to create a new coalition. Opposition fueled on such hopes is not likely to be united, useful, or important. In turn, the failure of opposition to coalesce throws the full weight of opposition upon components of the governmental coalition itself. Whether a government without an organized opposition, facing the only significant challenges from within its own ranks, can husband its energies sufficiently to pursue policy lines and maintain its own stability is a difficult question.

3. A major distinguishing factor between the advocates of proportional electoral systems and those of plurality electoral systems is their almost diametrically opposite assumptions about the character of the legislative process. For the proportionality advocate, the legislature approximates a mirror reflection of the society at the time of election, and by the first meeting of the legislature few if any of the societal cleavages will have been settled. As a natural consequence, the proportionally elected legislature is best described as an arena for the formation of coalitions behind policy rather than as an arena in which a partially preforged coalition is activated for policy making. Therefore, the proportional legislature will have a wider range of issues before it than will the plurality legislature, since in the plurality legislature the prescreening process of electoral coalition will reduce the number of legitimate questions at the same time that it produces greater policy stability in the assembly. Underlying these observations is the nature of the relationship between elections and legislative activity. The act of legislating for the proportionality advocate is separate from the act of electing: the election reproduces the society in the legislature while the act of legislating raises issues for this society writ small to consider. In a very real sense these become conceptually different processes. On the other hand, the plurality advocate sees the act of legislating as an extension of the act of electing, since the nomination, campaign, and election phase of electioneering have all been based around the formation of a coalition sufficiently strong to ensure local victory. Precisely because plurality election systems force the contenders to seek out like-minded partners in order to assure victory, the nature of the questions and in part the nature of the legislative answers are consciously forged before the legislature itself ever convenes. In that sense, it is conceptually much more difficult to separate the legislative aspect from the electoral aspect in plurality systems, perhaps accounting for the vast amount of research that has been done on the legislative process and constituency behavior in plurality systems.

3a. There are a number of corollary observations that flow

from this initial distinction. In the first place, if the proportional systems tend to duplicate the fissures in the society in the legislature, as a conceptually separate process from the act of policy making, the legislature itself is faced with two choices. It may, first, merely apply those fissures and cleavages to the legislative proposals at hand; and the legislators, upon discovering that such cleavages make legislative life intolerable, may do nothing. Or secondly, they may attempt to bridge over these disputes and create a coalition for policy making, although the elements of the coalition may be rather unstable. In any case, the most important question is whether the legislature will be able to forge a coalition that was not possible in the electoral campaign. In short, with proportional representation it is assumed that legislatures are the proper arena for the creation of policy coalitions and that there should be little, if any, prelegislative effort at coalition formation. With plurality systems the opposite is assumed, since the dynamics of the plurality system will by and large force an early coalition arrangement, either in the form of large, heterogeneous parties or at least working coalitions, such as the French Federation of the Left. Whether these arrangements are any more stable than those executed under proportionality may be questioned, but at least there is the possibility for some prelegislative policy negotiation, an important phase conspicuously absent from the proportional systems.

3b. This general observation can also create problems for the plurality advocate. Insofar as a society is deeply divided, particularly along geographic lines, plurality systems may create many more problems than they can solve. The assumption that large fissures in the society have been papered over in a prelegislative stage may be totally unwarranted; and if the legislature meets either with an understanding to ignore certain questions — for example, the questions of communal relations in Malaya — or with a policy coalition that has excluded certain volatile and important components of the society — for example, the American urban Negro — plurality has done a severe disservice to the policy process. On the other hand, if the legislature — and in a broader sense the whole government — is viewed as the agent through which basic cleavages in the society will be negotiated out of existence at the governmental level, and if that government is elected through a prescreening device such as plurality, the legislature and the whole governmental structure may fall apart, asked to do that which it cannot. It is perhaps useful to cite the Nigerian experience here, although the existence of federalism in that unhappy country was an additional complicating device. In such a case perhaps the only effective alternative is a system that combines a modified federalism, guaranteed representation for minorities, and pressures toward coalition building through a partial application of the plurality principle.

4. The legislative functions under plurality and proportionality are distinctly different processes, and the impact of this distinction is an important determinant of other institutional behavior. It follows that if the form of the electoral system has important implications for the workings of the legislature, it must also have implications for the working of the majority coalition, particularly in parliamentary regimes.

4a. Obviously, party discipline and ministerial stability are far greater under plurality because of the partial integration during the election phase. To a greater extent than under proportionality the legislative and governmental leadership will be known, as in the case of the parliamentary system, where the leadership of the major pretenders to power and the obvious coalition lines are observable in advance. With proportionality, given the difficulty of keeping electoral coalitions together (should any form), given the tendency for larger numbers of parties to find representation, and finally given the relatively more difficult task of maintenance, elite prediction is more difficult and more alternatives exist for the elite to expand and shift with whims in the legislature.

4b. By the same token, however, a breakdown in the linkage between the coalition in the legislature and the popular ideological distribution will have a far more severe impact on the plurality legislature than upon the proportional legislature, particularly if the latter has a larger number of parties. The elite in the plurality legislature will have been chosen by a prescreening process that may have substantially filtered out the very elements that now form the center of the societal distribution. Proportionality is far more likely to give representation to such a fledgling movement, and its greater range of alternatives in the legislature itself make the construction of a timely elite a more viable possibility. In this case the coalition pressures of plurality election systems may have obscured the growth of popular cleavages and contributed to the isolation of the legislature from the general policy requirements of the society.

4c. The character of the plurality coalition and its proportional counterpart has internal implications as well. Given the prescreened nature of the ideal plurality majority, party discipline and ministerial stability should be higher than in the comparable proportional legislature. But by the same token, since the stability of the legislative majority is expected to be higher than in a more heterogeneous legislature elected under proportionality, the impact of governmental fall will be considerably greater than under proportionality. To argue the same thing another way, the possibility of preresolution of societal tensions leads to assumptions about the stability of the legislature itself, and the cracking of this electoral coalition, sufficient to bring down a government in parliamentary regimes, is far more serious under plurality than under proportional systems. In the proportional system fissures of the society are expected in the legislature. In plurality systems, where the organizational stability made possible by the electoral coalition creates an image of permanence, the breaking of the coalition implies the inadequacy of the whole electoral-legislative coalition. Consequently, while governmental falls in parliamentary plurality regimes will be infrequent, they will also be far more serious than in the proportional systems.

5. The general character of the voter-party-legislature relationship is substantially different under the two broad types of electoral systems. Because the plurality model forces coalition building, there are more likely to be broad political (although unorganized) challenges that do not achieve representation. These unrepresented numbers will be added to

those excluded by other parties and their followers who have gathered their forces in coalition. As a result the voter in a plurality system may be faced more frequently with a demand that he cast his ballot as an affirmation of his faith in the political system rather than for policy preferences. As the number of voters participating for sheer system maintenance increases, the validity of the prelegislative coalition as a policy device in plurality legislatures is challenged and rendered less important. A plurality coalition is an effective policy device only so long as citizen commitments are largely instrumental and only secondarily systemic.

The general argument may be seen more clearly in terms of the exchange concept. In normal elections voters will cast their ballots for the party that comes closest to their own policy preferences, and in doing so, they will not support other parties and candidates who are further from their own perceived positions. For a gratifying party policy the voter exchanges his freedom to support other alternatives. In proportional systems, most clearly the list system, the voter is able to approximate closely his own policy positions because of the larger number of contenders and the relatively easier task of gaining representation. As in the French Fifth Republic, the problem becomes one of a higher order when the voter in majority systems is asked to support a coalition in an electoral district on the single ground that it will prevent the success of another group that is perceived as a threat to the entire political system. The voter is asked to make a qualitatively different kind of exchange in this process, for he is asked to support a coalition for reasons other than policy and only in the name of system maintenance. Insofar as the exchange process is one of system maintenance and not of policy exchanges, the prelegislative coalition can only claim to be one that is predisposed to hold the political system together, one in which there is little prior agreement on policy. An inadequate policy coalition in a legislature whose design and assumptions assume the existence of some sort of prescreening of social cleavage creates problems discussed in 3b above.

The distinction between policy exchanges and system main-

taining ones, clear from an examination of the French majority election system, applies to the pure plurality form of
election. It too forces interests to aggregate in order to prevent
a victory by a large plurality, asking voters to accept a narrower range of policy alternatives than proportional representation might afford. The dynamic at work is the same though
less obvious in extent. If, for example, a third-party candidate
in the Canadian West appears likely to gather 35 percent of
the vote based in a residential (and generally leftist) university
community, it behooves the two major parties either to come
to some sort of agreement or at least to suppress the possibility
that the major party vote will be further divided by the
emergence of a new party on the right. The same general
argument can be made in another context, the perceived
threat of parties of the German right against the established
political order of the Bonn Republic. In each of these cases
the normal fractionalization of the electorate would provide
a strong opportunity for a candidate whose inclinations favor
a restructuring of the social or political system. Supporters of
that order are now asked to accept a limited set of political
alternatives in order that their forces be concentrated behind
candidates whose credentials make them more acceptable to
the political establishment. In the process of electing such
candidates, however, the notion of policy coalition is discarded in favor of system maintenance, quite a different order
of political temper.

6. It is not only the legislature that is substantially affected
by the exclusive character of plurality and the representative
character of proportionality. The pressures within a society
that are denied access in their proportional influence may yet
have an opportunity to evade the legislative coalition and
obtain a hearing elsewhere in the political system. In particular, the channels of the bureaucracy may be open to specific
losers in the policy debate. In short, the concept of representative bureaucracy may be more consistent with plurality election than it is with the open representation characteristic of
proportional elections, and it may well be the bureaucracy
that establishes itself as the channel through which policy

positions outside the general policy coalition dominating the legislature are able to be heard. By the same token the strength of the executive, particularly a separate presidential form, may make it an agent of involvement with groups selected out by the coalition process during the elections, especially if a head of state is willing to use his office as a teaching lectern for the whole society.

Care must be exercised to separate the phenomenon of representative bureaucracy under plurality from a heightened executive under proportionality. Groups able to appeal to the bureaucracy as losers in the electoral coalition are able to do so only as advocates of positions whose rationality is forceful. They have little influence in the legislature and as a consequence are not able to bring extraordinary pressure to bear on any part of the executive that is not cooperative. They are in a true sense pleaders at the table, and whether the bureaucracy becomes an advocate of their cause is for that body alone to decide. Proportionality presents quite a different picture, since the general role of the executive may be vastly heightened by quarreling ineffectiveness on the part of the legislature attempting to pursue policy goals. At the end point, if the legislature is completely unable to agree on policy lines or, worse, on a set of ministers to govern, the tasks of administering the state become the tasks of policy formulation coincident with execution. The heightening of executive power in the presence of a legislature dominated by a negative majority is a political phenomenon of a totally different magnitude from representative bureaucracy under plurality regimes. In the latter case, the bureaucracy becomes advocate of a minority position, although admittedly the creation of effective clientele relationships has been known to be of use to agencies in the past.

7. It is in the area of ecology that the most important of the questions left unexplored by this volume can be found. Casually suggested in such discussions as those of Weimar Germany and the West German Republic, and found also in cases as widely diverse as Japan and Illinois, the general hypothesis might be pursued that it is the character of political

forces extant at the time of constitution writing that will determine the distance a polity can move toward the exclusiveness of plurality or toward the representation implicit in proportionality. Simply enough, were the memories of Weimar so fresh that West Germany could not adopt a scheme of proportional representation? Were the divisions in the German society so real that plurality would have left too many interests unrepresented? This explanation has barely been touched, and yet the interaction between election system and the environment which created it is perhaps the most important of all.

In simplest terms, throughout this volume election systems have been treated neither as completely dependent upon some other set of forces nor as completely independent variables. Rather, the election system is an intermediate variable able to influence the nature and behavior of institutions of government while itself being the target of other influences. The impact of the electoral system is in two linked stages. In the first place, and often unrecognized as an influence on the political system itself, the selection of the form of the electoral system is a dependent variable affected by a host of factors, not the least of which is the character of the society itself. A society in which large segments are strongly alienated from the general population, at the same time that they are not geographically isolated, probably will not be able to employ simple plurality as an electoral device. On the other hand, if a population is relatively homogeneous — has no deep internal conflicts — then the society probably will be able to employ with considerable success the plurality technique. It is certainly true that the history of socialist parties in Europe is a history of flirtation with proportional representation, while the history of those states in which ideological movements have had difficult going is one of plurality election. In these cases it is certainly a first hypothesis that the election system may not be an independent variable, but may be partially dependent upon the general character of the social system.

The second effect of the electoral system is in the development of the society itself. While social systems are dynamic, electoral systems are not, and to boot they are often creators of entrenched interests willing and able to defend the election device. Thus, while the society may evolve considerably beyond its initial phase, of either discord or unity, the electoral system that was initially the dependent variable may continue to reflect the initial state. In this form the electoral system in fact impedes the development of the society, when proportional systems act as a brake on the growth of unity and plurality systems act as a goad toward consensus. Additional recalcitrance is a product of policy makers whose political fortunes are in part linked with the form of election system to which they owe their political rise. It is these policy makers in turn who must support or at least tacitly not oppose the new election system changed social conditions might require. By means of this two-step, linked process the electoral system has its impact on the entire legislative system and to some degree on the entire political system.

It is from this last perspective that we see the tremendous potential of the electoral system as a generator of power for the legislature and, beyond its confines, for the whole governmental system. An electoral system which produces a legislative coalition attuned to the demands and needs of the population while providing a policy coalition that can produce results for the entire political system is capable of generating policy of enormous authority. In that sense policy capacity is generated for the legislature and for the government as a whole, since the policy process is able to extend and expand toward objectives perhaps otherwise proscribed. If, on the other hand, the electoral system creates a fundamentally ill-attuned legislative coalition, the capacity for performance is substantially reduced, and governmental power is lessened because governmental authority has been lessened. Authority means more than popularity. An unpopular coalition is lessened in its capacity by its inability to mobilize popular organizational support as well as popular acceptance. Insofar as the government has fewer active supporters in the population, force is required to gain its way, and there are fewer willing in the population to identify actively with the state. The end result is an approach to the politics of system survival and a movement away from the politics of system maintenance and of course systemic innovation. The effort expended in forced acceptability is further reductive of the available capacity of government. In these terms it can be argued that a well aligned electoral system and society produce a government able to expand its power and influence, an improperly aligned system reduces that capacity.

Appendix: Gaullism and the Apparentement—A 1951 Test of the 1962 Election Results in France

THE PURPOSES OF THE APPENDIX are to test the propositions that election systems do make a difference in election results and that the election system of the Fifth Republic actually made a considerable difference in the electoral outcome. In one and the same effort we hope to prove one thesis of the book — biases of structures — and to illustrate the impact of changes in the French voting law discussed in Chapter III.

It is difficult to separate the impact of the Gaullist presidency from the influence of the new electoral system in comparing the French electoral system of 1962 with the system of 1951. Both systems emphasized coalition, both systems required an absolute majority for success on the first ballot, and both systems seemed to punish extreme parties, particularly the Communists, when the necessary preconditions were present. But there were marked differences between the two systems, particularly the destructive effect on smaller parties. The 1951 electoral system had encouraged them to live within an alliance framework; the 1958 electoral system encouraged only those small parties able to survive without victory at the polls, namely, the party of blackmail. In order to suggest some of the contributions made by the Fifth Republic electoral system it is necessary "to conduct the election of 1962 [1] over again," that is, to recast the data in a manner that makes it possible to apply the apparentement of 1951. The assumptions involved are formidable — notably those about the nature of coalitions — but it is perhaps a useful exercise.

First, only four departments were carried by one party on its own, without coalition, and all of these were carried by the UNR. Secondly, if no alliance is assumed at all — that is, pure proportional representation by party is applied — no party gets more than about one-third of the seats, again a pattern similar to what probably would have happened in 1951. But if one can assume that the Gaullists are aided by one of the conservative parties — for example, the CNI — then the picture changes remarkably, especially if one assumes a coalition of the center in opposition. The results appear something like this:

Gaullist coalition wins by majority	15 departments	64 seats
Center coalition wins by majority	14 departments	41 seats
Total	29	105

The UNR wins only four departments on their own containing 24 seats, but in alliance with only one other group they are able to gain 40 seats; the center parties are able to win no departments individually by absolute majorities, but in coalition they win fourteen departments and 41 seats. In the Paris region the Gaullists (operating, it must be remembered, under proportional representation alone, without apparentement) win 29 more seats, added to their provincial victories, and the total number of Gaullist seats reaches 210. (But note that the CNI won 7 seats on its own so the total might actually read 217.) The center coalition wins a small number of Paris seats,

[1] 1962 was chosen rather than 1958 to escape, if at all possible, the dislocations of Algeria and the new impact of de Gaulle.

12, which, when added to its seats won by absolute majority
and its strength in the provinces, reaches a total of 159.

Gaullist alliance	210
CNI (Paris seats)	7
Independents	9
Center coalition	159
Communists	80
Total	465

Under the run-off system actually employed in the Fifth Republic the UNR alone won 229 seats, so that with its related
smaller parties a relatively comfortable majority could be ob-
tained. Had the electoral system of 1951 been in use, the best
that a Gaullist *alliance* might have done is about 13 seats
short of what the party *on its own* accomplished under the
run-off system of 1958; had the UNR alone been forced to
contest under apparentement, as indeed was largely the case
with its predecessor the RPF in 1951, the party would have
fallen well below 200 seats and there would have been little
chance of a majority in the Chamber of Deputies, much less
the relatively stable majority of the period after 1962.

Index